Hard Drives
Made Simple

Made Simple *Computer Books*

- easy to follow   • jargon free   • practical   • task based   • easy steps

Thousands of people have already discovered that the **MADE SIMPLE** series gives them what they want *fast!* These are the books for you if you want to **learn quickly what's essential** and **how** to do things with a particular piece of software. You are:

- **a Secretary** or **temp** who wants to **get the job done, quickly** and **efficiently**

- **a Manager**, without the time to learn all about the software but who wants to **produce letters, memos, reports** or **spreadsheets**

- someone **working from home**, who needs a **self-teaching** approach, that gives **results fast**, with the least confusion.

For **clarity** and **simplicity**, the **MADE SIMPLE** Computer Books stand above all others.

This **best selling** series is in your **local bookshop now**, or in case of difficulty, contact:

Reed Book Services Ltd., Orders Dept, PO Box 5, Rushden, Northants, NN10 9YX. Tel 0933 58521. Fax 0933 50284. Credit card sales 0933 410511.

Series titles:

Excel for Windows	Stephen Morris	0 7506 2070 6
Lotus 1-2-3 (DOS)	Ian Robertson	0 7506 2066 8
MS-DOS	Ian Sinclair	0 7506 2069 2
MS-Works for Windows	P. K. McBride	0 7506 2065 X
Windows 3.1	P. K. McBride	0 7506 2072 2
Word for Windows	Keith Brindley	0 7506 2071 4
WordPerfect (DOS)	Stephen Copestake	0 7506 2068 4
Access for Windows	Moira Stephen	0 7506 2309 8
The Internet	P.K.McBride	0 7506 2311 X
Quicken for Windows	Stephen Copestake	0 7506 2308 X
WordPerfect for Windows	Keith Brindley	. 0 7506 2310 1
Lotus 123 (5.0) for Windows	Stephen Morris	0 7506 2307 1
Multimedia	Simon Collin	0 7506 2314 4
Pageplus for Windows	Ian Sinclair	0 7506 2312 8
Powerpoint	Moira Stephen	0 7506 2420 5
Hard Drives	Ian Robertson	0 7506 2313 6
Windows 95	P.K. McBride	0 7506 2306 3
WordPro	Moira Stephen	0 7506 2626 7
Microsoft Office 95	P.K. McBride	0 7506 2625 9

Hard Drives
Made Simple

Ian Robertson

MADE SIMPLE
BOOKS

Made Simple
An imprint of Butterworth-Heinemann Ltd
Linacre House, Jordan Hill, Oxford OX2 8DP

ᴿ A member of the Reed Elsevier plc group

OXFORD   LONDON   BOSTON
MUNICH   NEW DELHI   SINGAPORE   SYDNEY
TOKYO   TORONTO   WELLINGTON

First published 1995
© Ian Robertson1995

TRADEMARKS/REGISTERED TRADEMARKS
Computer hardware and software brand names mentioned in this book are protected
by their respective trademarks and are acknowledged.

British Library Cataloguing in Publication Data
A catalogue record for this book is available from the British Library

ISBN 0 7506 2313 6

Design and Typeset by P.K.McBride, Southampton

Archetype, Bash Casual, Cotswold and Gravity fonts from Advanced Graphics Ltd
Icons designed by Sarah Ward © 1994
Printed and bound in Great Britain by Scotprint, Musselburgh, Scotland

Contents

Preface

The computer is about as simple as a spacecraft, and who ever let an untrained spaceman loose? You pick up a manual that weighs more than your birth-weight, open it and find that its written in computerspeak. You see messages on the screen that look like code and the thing even makes noises. No wonder that you feel it's your lucky day if everything goes right. What do you do if everything goes wrong? Give up.

Training helps. Being able to type helps. Experience helps. This book helps, by providing training and assisting with experience. It can't help you if you always manage to hit the wrong keys, but it can tell you which are the right ones and what to do when you hit the wrong ones. After some time, even the dreaded manual will start to make sense, just because you know what the writers are wittering on about.

Computing is not black magic. You don't need luck or charms, just a bit of understanding. The problem is that the programs that are used nowadays look simple but aren't. Most of them are crammed with features you don't need – but how do you know what you don't need? This book shows you what is essential and guides you through it. You will know how to make an action work and why. The less essential bits can wait – and once you start to use a program with confidence you can tackle these bits for yourself.

The writers of this series have all been through it. We know your time is valuable, and you don't want to waste it. You don't buy books on computer subjects to read jokes or be told that you are a dummy. You want to find what you need and be shown how to achieve it. Here, at last, you can.

1 Why use a hard drive?

Hard and floppy

The floppy type of disk has several limitations. The main limitation is that the disk spends most of its life out of the drive, subject to the dust and smoke in the room where the disk is housed. The recording and replaying heads are in contact with the disk surface, so that the disk cannot be spun at a very high speed because of the friction of the heads and of the sleeve which partially protects it.

The hard drive is a way of obtaining a much larger amount of information packed into the normal size of a disk. The disks (called *platters*) and their magnetic read/write heads are permanently sealed inside a container that ensures a dust-free environment for the drive. The diagram shows a set of platters cut away to that the heads are visible.

❑ Hard disks hold more information, typically several hundred times more than a floppy.

❑ You can keep all your programs and data on a hard drive; no need to look for floppies and insert them.

❑ You can boot the computer from the hard drive rather than from a special floppy.

❑ Hard drives are much faster than floppies.

❑ You can store programs that would not fit on a floppy.

❑ You can organise your files more sensibly.

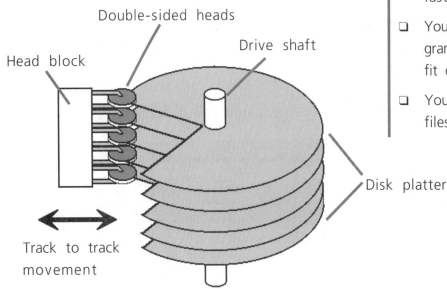

Double-sided heads

Drive shaft

Head block

Disk platter

Track to track movement

2

The down side

- [ ] A hard disk can fail gradually, giving you time to backup, or it may fail suddenly.

- [ ] The larger the size of hard disk, the more careful you need to be about backing up.

- [ ] After some use, a hard drive can become cluttered with un-wanted files. Some housekeeping is always needed.

- [ ] A virus on a hard drive is much more serious than one on a floppy. You can afford to throw away a floppy disk that has a virus – you can't afford to scrap a hard drive.

- [ ] If your computer is stolen, all the contents of the hard drive will go with it. You can insure the computer, but you can't insure the data on your hard drive.

Damage

The most common cause of damage to a hard disk is physical knocking that causes the drive heads to come into violent contact with the platters. The risk is much greater if the machine is jolted while the drive is being used, because in normal action, the head flies over each platter side with a separation of only a few millionths of an inch.

A jolt while the machine is operating can therefore cause a score to be cut into the coating of one or more platters, causing irreparable damage.

Modern hard disk units park the heads safely over an unused track (the last on each platter) when the machine is switched off, and some computers contain firmware (in the ROM) which parks disk heads automatically when the machine has not been used for a minute or so.

Don't move your computer while it is running, and try to avoid knocking against it. Don't over-react – it takes a really violent knock to be certain of damaging a drive, but no-one wants to be the first to discover just how hard you need to hit your computer to cause damage.

Take note

The most important thing in hard-drive life is making backups. All else is detail.

Finding the size

You have just bought a new computer. How do you find out about the hard drive? Does it work? Was it correctly set-up? Is it the size the salesman said it is? What's on it?

You can find out the size of the hard drive on a modern computer by using a utility called MSD. Type the commands:

```
CD C:\DOS
MSD
```

and when the menu appears move the mouse cursor to the portion labelled 'Disk Drives' and click the mouse button. The display will show all the drives, and the C: drive is the hard drive. In a typical display, below, the size of the hard drive and the amount of free space is shown. The hard drive illustrated here is of 244 Mbyte capacity with only 12M free. Time to do some re-organising!

❏ When a computer has been correctly set up, it will load in files automatically, with messages on the screen. Finally it will show the message C:>, or start Windows, or start some other program.

❏ If your computer starts and runs DOS, you can find out about the hard drive by using the program MSD, as shown here.

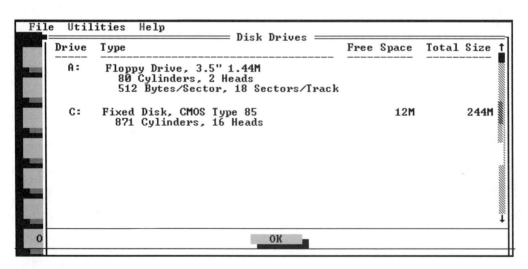

```
 File   Utilities   Help
                                  ═══ Disk Drives ═══
     Drive   Type                              Free Space   Total Size  ↑
     ─────   ────                              ──────────   ──────────
      A:     Floppy Drive, 3.5" 1.44M
             80 Cylinders, 2 Heads
             512 Bytes/Sector, 18 Sectors/Track

      C:     Fixed Disk, CMOS Type 85               12M          244M
             871 Cylinders, 16 Heads




                                                                        ↓
   0                          ▢ OK ▢
```

The A: drive is always a floppy; the C drive is always the hard drive.

Disk sizes

Disk size is measured in megabytes, abbreviated to Mb. 1 Mb is 1024 Kbytes, and 1 Kbyte is 1024 bytes. If you think of one byte as the storage space for one character then a hard drive of 244 Mbyte has space for 255.8 million characters. That's about 800,000 A4 pages of text.

Disk size in Windows

If you use Windows, you can find the size of your hard drive by using File Manager. The size of the drive and the amount that is free is printed at the foot of the File Manager display.

This display also shows the size of files in the current directory. In the illustration, the C: directory is in use, so that directory size that is shown is for this directory.

This example shows a much larger hard drive — or so it appears. It is, in fact, the same drive, and the difference is caused by using the MS-DOS utility, DriveSpace.

Take note

A computer may claim 500 Mb of space, but the hard drive is of 244 to 300 Mb and DriveSpace has been used. In practice, the capacity depends on the type of files stored.

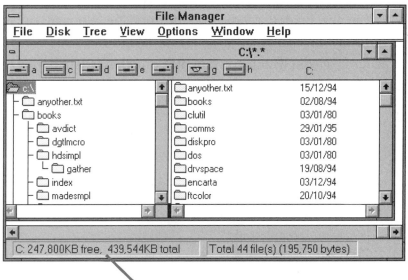

Finding the size and free space in WIndows 3.1...

... and in Windows 95

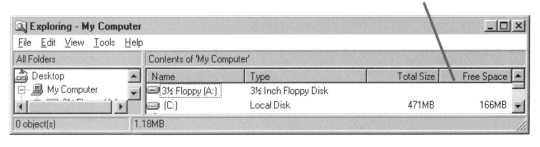

Directories

A directory is a collection of files, and the use of directories is a way of making it easier to use a hard drive.

You can think of a directory as being a sort of disk full of files, with the difference that you have immediate access to all of these directories; they do not have to be inserted and removed like floppy disks.

Windows uses symbols to indicate the type of file and to indicate a directory. You can run a program, for example, by double-clicking on its filename. If you double-click on the name of a data file you *might* find that this has the effect of running the program that created the data file, with the file loaded ready for editing. The alternative (Windows 3.1) is an error message, or (Windows 95) a list of programs from which you can pick one that will use the data file.

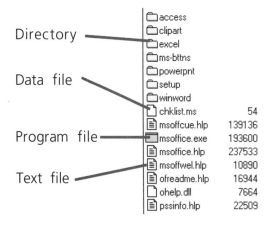

Window icons

A directory on a File Manager display is indicated by a symbol like a folder

This symbol is for a data file which might be text or graphics.

This symbol is for a program file, one that you can run and which might create data

Tip

Learn to recognise these symbols, as they allow you to read your directory display quickly.

Organisation

❑ The tree diagram is one way of thinking about the organisation of your files, but how you arrange your tree is entirely up to you.

❑ You might want to use a directory for a word-processor, and subdirectories (branches) for all the different kinds of text files that you create – letters, invoices, receipts and so on.

❑ You might, by contrast, prefer to keep more than one word processor in a main directory, and have quite separate directories (coming off the main stem) for different types of text.

❑ The important point is that you should create a directory structure that suits you.

Directory trees

The conventional way of thinking of a set of directories is as the roots of a tree. The main stem (or root) is used to represent the main directory, the one that holds all others. For a hard drive this is directory C:\; for a floppy it would be A:\. Other directories or sub-directories are shown as minor rootlets branching from this main one.

On paper it looks like this:

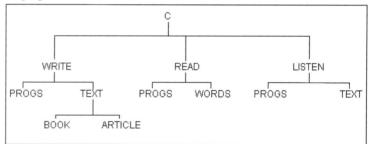

By contrast, look at the system below. Everything is put into four directories that are all attached to the root. This will cause problems like clashing filenames (you can't have two files of the same name in the same directory) and file mixtures (all the data files in one directory).

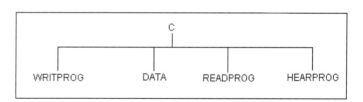

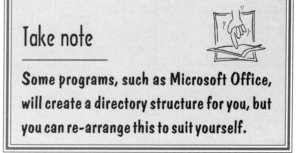

Take note

Some programs, such as Microsoft Office, will create a directory structure for you, but you can re-arrange this to suit yourself.

Trees and roots

You should keep a printed tree diagram to see your directory structure. Oddly enough, it's much easier using DOS than Windows - see the steps.

In DOS, you use the MS-DOS utility TREE.COM, which will be in the C:\DOS directory. If your computer is correctly set up with a PATH line (see later) you can simply type TREE – but you will probably find that the result is too much to fit on the screen.

Get around this by using the command TREE | MORE, or better still, print the whole diagram on paper. With your printer switched on and loaded with paper, type:

TREE > PRN

and wait until the printer finishes. You might need to glue several sheets of paper together unless you are using continuous paper with a dot-matrix printer.

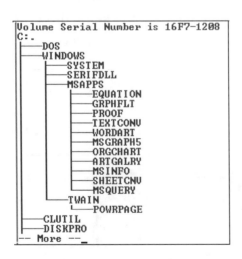

```
Volume Serial Number is 16F7-1208
C:.
├──DOS
├──WINDOWS
│      ├──SYSTEM
│      ├──SERIFDLL
│      ├──MSAPPS
│      │      ├──EQUATION
│      │      ├──GRPHFLT
│      │      ├──PROOF
│      │      ├──TEXTCONV
│      │      ├──WORDART
│      │      ├──MSGRAPH5
│      │      ├──ORGCHART
│      │      ├──ARTGALRY
│      │      ├──MSINFO
│      │      ├──SHEETCNV
│      │      └──MSQUERY
│      └──TWAIN
│             └──POWRPAGE
├──CLUTIL
├──DISKPRO
-- More --_
```

□ **Windows 3.1**

1 Enter File Manager.

2 Find the DOS directory and the TREE.COM program.

3 Use the **File–Run** option in File Manager

4 Type the **TREE > PRN** command and wait for the printer to complete the action.

□ **Windows 95**

1 Display your tree diagram using **Explorer** or **File Manager** and press **[Print Screen]** to capture the image.

2 Open **Paint** and use **Edit – Paste** to copy in the diagram.

3 Use **File – Print** to send it to your printer.

4 If your tree diagram is a large one, you will have to repeat these steps, scrolling down the Explorer or File Manager window.

Parts

- ❑ The main stem is the left-most vertical line. For the hard drive this represents the root directory C:\

- ❑ The names that are shown in the tree display are all of directories.

- ❑ When one directory branches from another, the display shows a stub of vertical line to indicate the level of the directory – the further over this is to the right the lower the level.

- ❑ You have to decide for yourself how deep to plant your directories. On one hand you need to follow a logical arrangement, on the other hand you need to avoid having to have too many layers.

Reading the TREE

Both Windows File Manager and the DOS TREE display give the same type of diagram, in which the leftmost vertical line is the root, and all other directories are shown to the right of this.

You can see in a display like this that one directory can branch from another. You are allowed to have directories stacked up to eight deep in this way, but it's unusual to need more than three layers of sub-directories.

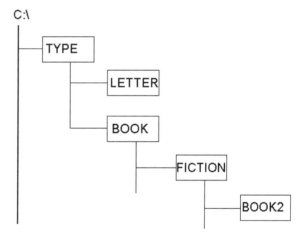

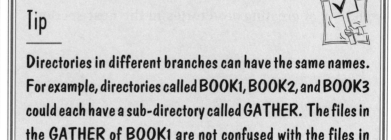

Tip

Directories in different branches can have the same names. For example, directories called BOOK1, BOOK2, and BOOK3 could each have a sub-directory called GATHER. The files in the GATHER of BOOK1 are not confused with the files in GATHER of BOOK2.

Parent and child

The idea of *Parent* and *Child* is another useful way of working with directories. A child directory means a sub-directory of a parent. You can think of the root directory as being the parent of each directory that comes straight from the root.

In the same way, any other directory that has a sub-directory is its parent.

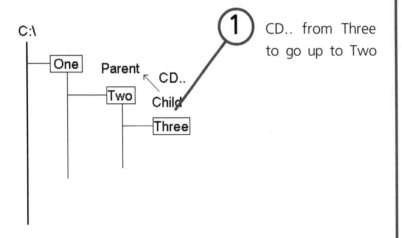

1 CD.. from Three to go up to Two

1 In DOS you can move from the child directory to its parent by using the command:

CD..

(**CD** followed by two dots, then **[Enter]**)

Using Windows, of course, you just click on the directory that you want, and you can select a directory to be a parent when you want to create a new child directory – we'll look at creating directories in the next section.

Tip

The CD.. command is a very fast and useful one, particularly if you cannot remember what the parent directory was called. It's also a very useful command to use in batch files if you create such files for yourself.

Basic steps

1 If the directory you want to make current is further down the same branch as your present directory, use **CD** followed by the names of the directories up to and including the one you want.

2 If the directory you want is on another branch, use **CD ** to get back to the root and continue with the names in the new branch, placing a backslash (\) between the names.

❑ The part of the command that follows CD in these examples is the *path*.

Paths

A path is a route from one directory to another. If you use Windows you don't need to worry too much about paths, because you can simply click on the name of the directory that you want to make current. It's a very different story if you use DOS.

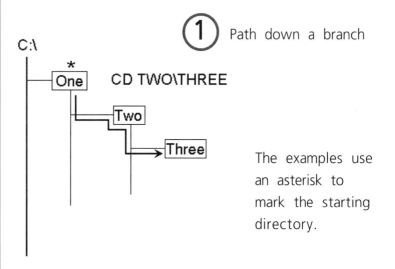

① Path down a branch

CD TWO\THREE

The examples use an asterisk to mark the starting directory.

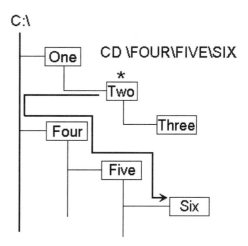

② Path up to the root then down

CD \FOUR\FIVE\SIX

11

Summary

❑ A hard drive is essential for a modern computer, mainly because programs are so large now and generate so many data files.

❑ A hard drive will die some day. Your preparation for this takes the form of **backups** on floppy disks or on a tape streamer.

❑ You can find **how much spac**e your hard drive can offer by using the MSD utility from DOS or the File Manager from Windows. Beware of the hard drive whose size has been quoted after using DriveSpace.

❑ A **Directory** (or Folder) is used to contain a group of files, preferably files of the same type, or related in some way. As viewed in Windows File Manager, or Windows 95 Explorer, the icon shapes indicate directories and types of files.

❑ The DOS **TREE** command will show the arrangement of directories. It's useful to print a copy of the directory tree so that you know how your directories are arranged. Printing is much simpler from DOS than from Windows 95.

❑ In any tree diagram, the **root** is to the left hand side. Levels of branching are indicated by their distance to the right.

❑ A **Path** is a route from one directory to another, and is used to change the current directory or to specify the directory for running a program.

2 Working with DOS

DOS

DOS or MS-DOS is the older system for running programs and organising files. Most of today's computer users are likely to use Windows rather than DOS, and if you use only Windows, particularly if you use Windows 95, you can skip this section altogether.

If you want to know how to use DOS, see the companion book in this set, DOS Made Simple.

If you are using an older version of DOS (50 or 6.0) you will have a program called DOSSHELL. This allows you to use DOS in a way that is similar to the methods of Windows, and its use makes working with had drive directories much easier.

DOSSHELL is not covered in this book because it is no longer supplied except to order.

Take note

What you can or cannot use is determined by the type of machine you have and how much memory you can use. If your PC is a 286 (or even an 8086 or 8088) then you should use DOS 5.0 and if you like it, DOSSHELL.

If your PC is a 386 and has 4 Mbyte of memory you can use Windows 3.1, but if you have only 1 or 2 Mbyte of memory, use DOS (and DOSSHELL optionally)

If your PC is a 486 or Pentium type with 8 Mbyte or more of memory, you can use Windows 95 and ignore DOS altogether.

DOS in Windows

❏ You can run DOS programs from within Windows 3.1 or Windows 95. You can also leave either of the Windows systems so that you can use DOS directly.

❏ When you leave Windows 3.1 you will automatically be returned to DOS.

❏ When you leave Windows 95 you can take the option of starting up DOS.

❏ You can start DOS before Windows 95 starts. Just press [F8] when you see the message about starting Windows 95, then use the menu that allows you to run DOS.

Basic steps

1 Type **CD C:\ [Enter]**

2 Type **DIR | MORE**

3 A list appears. The names in brackets are of directories. Each can hold many files.

4 The other names, with no brackets, are of files. You should have only a few files in the C:\ directory (the root)

5 You can also type the command in the form:

DIR /W

to display the list in a wide format.

6 Another option is:
DIR > PRN
which will print your directory display if your printer is ready.

What's on the disk?

You can find out what is on the hard drive using the DOS DIR command. The steps here illustrate how to show the contents of your hard drive using method, and all the rest of this section will be about using DOS.

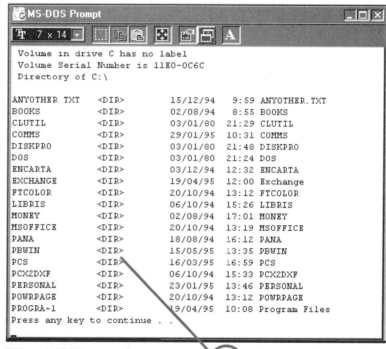

DIR | MORE seen in
Windows 95 DOS prompt

③ Directories

④ Files

① CD C:\ to go to the root

⑤ Type DIR \W

DIR \W in Windows 3.1
DOS prompt

Changing directory

If you want to make a sub-directory current, so that you can get to its stored files easily, you use the CD command. While you can move straight to any directory by typing in its full path (route through the tree), it is always simplest to work from the top down.

Suppose that you want to make your GETIT directory current, and it's arranged like this:

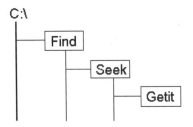

1 Type **CD ** to take you back to the root.

2 Type **CD FIND** to get to the first directory.

3 Type **CD SEEK** to get to the second level.

4 Type **CD GETIT** to get to the one you want.

❑ The alternative is to combine all these steps into one, and type:

  CD C:\FIND\SEEK\GETIT

  which will get you to the directory in one step – if you know how to find it. If in doubt, use one step at a time, and use a **DIR** command to make certain that you know where to go next.

Take note

You don't always need to make a directory current in order to use it. For example, WORD allows you to set a directory for text files, so that this will be used automatically for saving and loading when you are using WORD.

Tip

Place your data files in sub-directories that come directly off those that contain the programs that create the files. This makes it much easier to get to the files you need.

Tip

To find out about the DOS commands for moving, copying and deleting files, see DOS Made Simple. This book concentrates on commands that are specifically relevant to a hard drive.

Basic steps

1 Find the directory that you want to use as the parent, and make this current. In the example, the current directory is called ANOTHER.TXT.

2 Type the command starting with MD; e.g.:

MD MYNEWDIR

3 Press **[Enter]** to create the new directory.

This makes a directory called MYNEWDIR.

Take note

Creating a directory does not make it the current one. If you have created MYNEWDIR you need to use CD MYNEWDIR to make it the current directory.

Making a new directory

When you work in DOS, you need to take more care over how you create a directory. The command is MKDIR, usually abbreviated to MD, and it is followed (after a space) by the name of the directory that you want to create.

The rules for the directory name are the same as for a filename, a maximum of eight characters, and you can use an extension of up to three characters. Use only letters of the alphabet, digits and the hyphen (-) or underscore (_), no others

When the new directory has been created, it will appear in a TREE diagram and you can then start to use it.

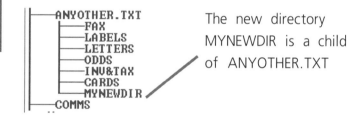

The new directory MYNEWDIR is a child of ANYOTHER.TXT

Tip

Always check your TREE diagram before you create a directory. This allows you to have second thoughts about which directory to use as the parent, and what to call the directory. Don't make decisions at the keyboard!

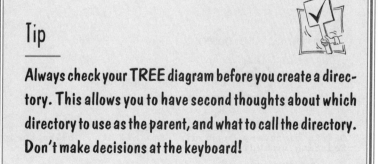

Deleting directories

The older DOS versions used the RMDIR command, abbreviated to RD, followed by the name of the directory to be deleted.

This command would not work if:

● the directory contained any sub-directories or files,

● you were currently using that directory.

Modern MS-DOS versions (6.1 onwards) contain the DELTREE command. This will delete a directory and everything it contains, files and sub-directories included. Unless you have full backups on floppy disks, it can be very difficult to recover anything after using DELTREE.

The examples show the commands in use and the DOS reminder that follows them.

(1) Empty the directory

(2) CD ..

(3) Remove the directory

```
C:\UTILS>rd notsouse.ful
C:\UTILS>
```

(1) Go to the parent

(2) Delete the directory

```
C:\ANYOTHER.TXT>deltree mynewdir
Delete directory "mynewdir" and all its subdirectories? [yn] y
Deleting mynewdir...

C:\ANYOTHER.TXT>_
```

(3) Confirm it

❏ RMDIR

1 Remove all the files from the directory to be deleted.

2 Use **CD ..** to go up to its parent directory.

3 Type **RD** followed by a space and the name of the directory then press [Enter].

4 To check that the directory has been removed, use **DIR** to view the contents of the current directory.

❏ DELTREE

1 Go to the parent of the directory to be deleted

2 Type DELTREE and the directory name.

3 When asked to confirm, type **Y** and press [Enter].

18

Basic steps

1 Open your AUTOEXEC.BAT file for editing.

2 At any convenient point, add the line:

SET DIRCMD=

and follow the = sign with the letters that indicate the type of files and sort order.

For example,

SET DIRCMD=/a:s

includes system files

SET DIRCMD=/o:gn

sorts directories ahead of files, using alphabetical order for both directories and files.

DOS directory display

The default arrangement of files for the DIR command is simply the order in which the files were added to the hard drive. If you want to show sorted directories you must add a DIRCMD line to your AUTOEXEC.BAT file.

DIRCMD uses symbols and letters to indicate what to list.

To start with **/a** will list files with specified attributes indicates by a colon and another letter. Note that if you use a – sign before a letter this has the meaning of NOT.

/a:a Files ready to backup (:–a no backup needed)

/a:d Directories included in list (:–d not included)

/a:h Include hidden files (:–h not included)

/a:s Include system files (:–s not included)

The **/o** set controls the sort order

/o:c Sort by compression ratio, low to high (:–c opposite)

/o:d Date and time, oldest first (:–d newest first)

/o:e Order of extension (:–e reverse order)

/o:g List directories belore files

/o:n Order of name (:–s reverse order:–n reverse order)

/o:s Order of file size (:–s reverse order)

Tip

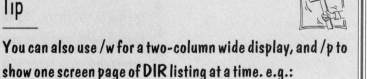

You can also use /w for a two-column wide display, and /p to show one screen page of DIR listing at a time. e.g.:

   SET DIRCMD=/w

will display a wide listing one page at a time

Paths in filenames

A path can be a very important part of a filename. There are, for example, two main ways of running a program, using DOS. You can opt to change to the directory that contains the program, making it current, and then typing the program name and pressing [Enter].

The alternative is to include a path to the program as part of the command, so that the program name comes last in the path. This is faster, but you need to know the path in advance – and get all the spelling correct in one go.

Basic steps

1 Type the **CD** line that makes the program's directory current.

2 Type the name and press **[Enter]** to run the program.

Or

3 Type the full path as part of the command to run the program.

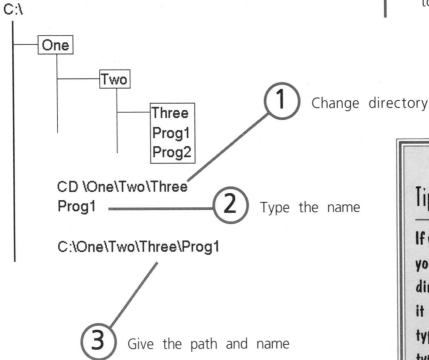

C:\

One

Two

Three
Prog1
Prog2

CD \One\Two\Three
Prog1

C:\One\Two\Three\Prog1

1 Change directory

2 Type the name

3 Give the path and name

Tip

If you are uncertain, find your way to the correct directory first. If you get it wrong, you need less typing to get there. If you type the whole path as one command, one error will require you to edit or re-type the whole command.

Search order

- If there is no PATH in the AUTOEXEC.BAT file, the system searches in this order:

1 the current directory ;

2 the root directory, which might be a floppy root if you are currently using a floppy.

- No other directories are searched.

Take note

When you install some programs, they will alter the AUTOEXEC.BAT file and add to the PATH line. You need to check this at intervals to make sure that the PATH line does not become too large, slowing down search actions.

Path in AUTOEXEC.BAT

The AUTOEXEC.BAT file is used when DOS loads, and because Windows 3.1 uses DOS it also uses the information in the AUTOEXEC.BAT file. Windows-95 is different. If you are using Windows-95 see the Made Simple book for this system.

You can include in the AUTOEXEC.BAT file a line that starts with PATH which will direct DOS to search for program files in a specified set of directories, using a specified order. Windows 3.1 will add its own directory to the PATH line in your AUTOEXEC.BAT file when you install Windows. MS-DOS will usually create a line that includes C:\ and C:\DOS.

```
@ECHO OFF
SET BLASTER=A220 I5 D1 H5 P330 T6 > NUL
SET SOUND=C:\SB16
C:\SB16\SB16SET /M:220 /VOC:220 /CD:220 /MIDI:220 /LINE:220
C:\SB16\SBCONFIG.EXE /S > NUL
PROMPT $p$g
PATH C:\DOS;C:\WINDOWS;C:\
SET TEMP=C:\temp
LH /L:1,38208 C:\dos\mouse.com /y
LH /L:1,6384 C:\DOS\doskey/insert
set dircmd=/w/p/o:gn
LH /L:1,16656 C:\DOS\KEYB UK,,C:\DOS\KEYBOARD.SYS
LH /L:1,16944 C:\DOS\SHARE.EXE /L:500 /f:5100
LH /L:1,27952 C:\DOS\MSCDEX.EXE /D:MSCD000 > NUL
LH /L:0 C:\DOS\SMARTDRV.EXE
win
```

Path

Here, the C:\DOS directory will be searched first, followed by C:\WINDOWS, and finally by C:\.

Tip

See MS-DOS Made Simple if all this is new to you.

Picking your path

When you are working in DOS, the PATH line affects only program files (EXE and COM, also BAT). It does not affect text or other data files. This is easily forgotten, and you might find yourself typing something like:

TYPE MYFILE.TXT

forgetting that MYFILE is not in the current directory.

You should always provide a path along with a filename for a data file unless the data is in the current directory. The alternative is to use the DOS APPEND command in the AUTOEXEC.BAT file.

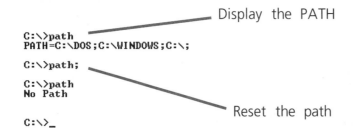

Display the PATH

```
C:\>path
PATH=C:\DOS;C:\WINDOWS;C:\;

C:\>path;

C:\>path
No Path

C:\>_
```

Reset the path

Take note

Do NOT use APPEND if you also use Windows.

❑ The different directory paths in a PATH line are separated by semicolons.

❑ The command **PATH** will display the current path list on the screen, so that you do not need to display the whole of your AUTOEXEC.BAT file.

❑ The command **PATH;** (with a semicolon at the end) will reset the path, so that only the current directory and its root will be searched. If you then use **PATH** by itself you will see the message **No Path**. This is sometimes useful if you want to ensure that you are reminded if a program is not in the current directory or the root.

Do and Don't

- ❏ DO check your directory tree before you add a new directory

- ❏ DON'T put any files on your root drive unless they must be there - and very few do.

- ❏ DO be very careful with DELTREE – once again, check your directory tree.

- ❏ DON'T forget backups. Some day you will need them.

- ❏ DO make use of DIRCMD. It's always easier to find files in a sorted directory than an unsorted one.

Odds and Ends

You can use the slash sign at the start of a pathname to mean the root directory, so that typing:

    \PAINTIT\MYDRAW

means that you want to run a program called MYDRAW which is in the C:\PAINTIT directory.

You can set up directories on floppy disks as well as on hard drives. The usual reason for this is to keep files separate, particularly if you have two sets of files with the same names (like FIG3_2.PCX) but which belong to different sets.

If you change your mind about a directory name you can re-name it. For example, if you have a directory which is C:\RUBBISH you can move to the C:\ root and type:

    REN RUBBISH NOTSOBAD

which will change the name to C:\NOTSOBAD

On older versions of MS-DOS then REN command could not be used this way, but the MOVE command could, using, for example:

    MOVE RUBBISH NOTSOBAD

Summary

❑ You are **forced to use** DOS if your computer is old or slow, or with limited memory. You might **prefer to use** DOS, though that makes you one of a minority these days.

❑ The hard drive is referred to as the **root** directory. Since the root can hold a maximum of 128 files, you should keep almost all of your files in directories.

❑ You use the **CD** command to move from one directory to another.

❑ You use the **MD** command to make a new (child) directory.

❑ You can use **RD** or **DELTREE** to delete a directory. DELTREE will also delete the sub-directories of a directory, and needs to be used with care.

❑ You can set **directory displays** to be sorted in order, to use the full screen width, and other options by using DIRCMD in the AUTOEXEC.BAT file.

❑ You often need to specify a **path** in the filename of a program in order to run the program.

❑ You can use a **PATH line** in the AUTOEXEC.BAT file to ensure that the named directories will be searched when you type a program name.

3 The Windows way

Going there

Getting to the directory that you want and making it current, is simple enough if you are using Windows and know where you want to go. Double-click on the first layer of directory, then on the next and so on until you find the one you want.

If you don't know where to find directories, you need to start by displaying all the directory layers, as noted in the Steps column.

1 Run **File Manager**.

2 From the **Tree** menu, select **Expand All**.

3 You will see all of the directories displayed. You may need to scroll up or down this display to find the one you want.

4 Click on this directory name to see its files listed in the right-hand side of the File Manager display.

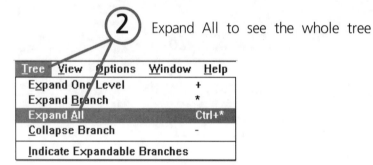

Expand All to see the whole tree

Tree	View	Options	Window	Help
Expand One Level				+
Expand Branch				*
Expand All				Ctrl+*
Collapse Branch				-
Indicate Expandable Branches				

Tip

If you have arranged your directories logically you will always know how to get to a directory - for example that LETTERS was a directory from WRITE.

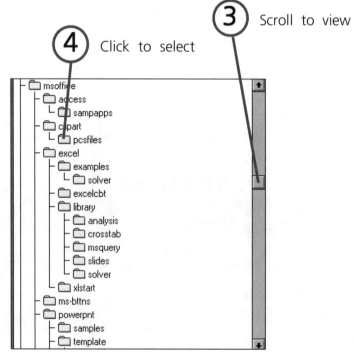

Scroll to view

Click to select

Basic steps

1 Click on the **Start** button of Windows 95 and move the cursor to **Programs** and then to **Windows Explorer**. Click on Explorer to open it window.

2 Click on the [+] sign next to the C drive to show the contents of the hard drive.

3 If you click on the [-] box the sub-folders will be hidden.

4 You can make a folder current by clicking on it, so that its files and sub-folders appear in the list on the right.

① Close sub-folders

Take note

Windows 95 uses the word **folder** to mean directory.

Explorer

Windows 95 can use File Manager if this program has been set up – see *Windows 95 Made Simple* for details of adding a program to the Start menu. You are encouraged, however, to use Windows Explorer instead.

At first, Explorer looks just like File Manager, but there are some important differences.

● The list on the left includes all drives, along with items such as the Recycle Bin, Desktop and My Computer.

● There is a single window which you use for all your file transfer work

● Folders (directories) and files are shown as icons, with the [+] box used to expand a folder (click on the + sign to expand.

② Click to expand

④ Click to make current

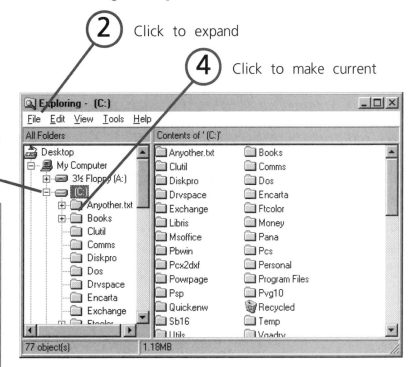

27

Making paths

Paths are often needed in Windows programs, so don't assume that you can forget about paths if you never use DOS directly. However, you can use the Browse action to supply the path for you, see next page.

For example, users of Microsoft Word can supply paths to specify where certain files can be found – this allows Word to find files automatically and you supply the information once only.

1 Using either version of Windows, you can locate a program file in File Manager and double-click on the name.

2 You can also find the file using Windows 95 Explorer, and double-click on the name.

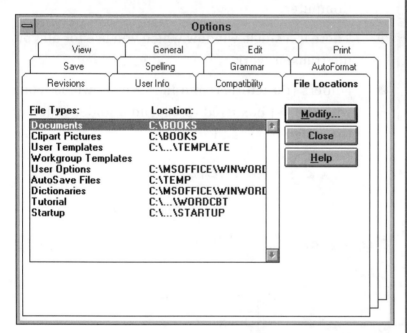

This shows the **Tools – Options – File locations** display of WORD, with the file locations shown as paths. You do not have to type the paths, however, only click on the directory you want after clicking on **Modify** or **New**.

Tip

Take a look at **Windows 95 Made Simple** to find out how to make a shortcut on the **Start** menu.

Basic steps

❑ **Making a program icon**

1 From Program Manager, click on **File** and then **New**.

2 The default is **Program Item**. Click on **OK** to see the Properties window.

3 *Either* press Browse to find the file and click to capture its name and path

Or type the path if you know it.

4 The **Command Line** is the full name of the program, including its path and extension.

5 The **Working Directory** shows the path to any data files that the program creates.

The easiest way to run a Windows 3.1 program is to use File Manager to locate the program file, and then double-click on the file name.

You might, however, want to add a program you often use into a Group that runs from Program Manager of Windows 3.1.

Similarly, you can create a shortcut in the Start menu of Windows 95 (not illustrated here).

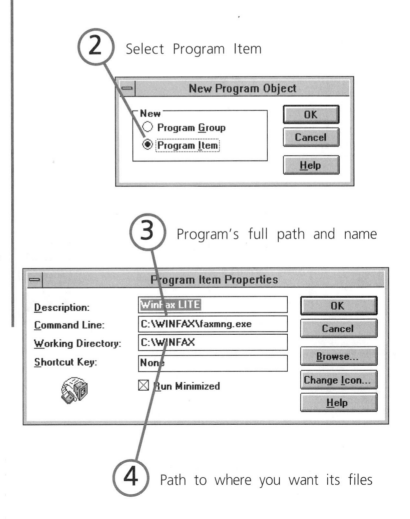

② Select Program Item

③ Program's full path and name

④ Path to where you want its files

Making a directory

Using Windows 3.1, making a new directory is simple. You work, as usual, in File Manager, picking the directory that will be the parent of the new one.

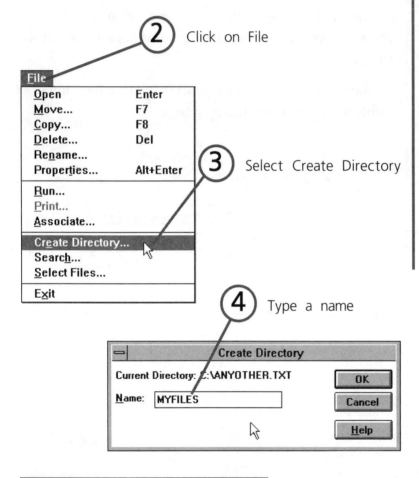

(2) Click on File

(3) Select Create Directory

(4) Type a name

1 Click on the directory which will be the parent of the one you want to create.

2 Open the **File** menu.

3 Click on **Create Directory**. You will see the dialog box appear.

4 Type in the name that you want to use.

❑ You will see the new directory name appear in the File Manager window.

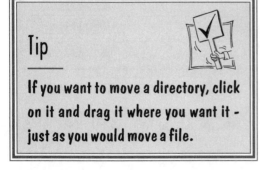

Tip

If you want to move a directory, click on it and drag it where you want it - just as you would move a file.

Take note

If the standard eight characters are not enough, you can add an extension to a name, making names such as **2GOOD2BE.TRU**, for example.

Basic steps

1 Place the pointer on the name of the folder you want to be the parent and click.

2 Click on the **File** menu, and move the pointer to **New**.

3 Select **Folder**.

4 You will see the folder appear, labelled *New Folder*. Edit this to create the required name.

Making a Windows 95 folder

The procedure for creating a new folder in Explorer is simple, but very different from the methods used in Windows 3.1.

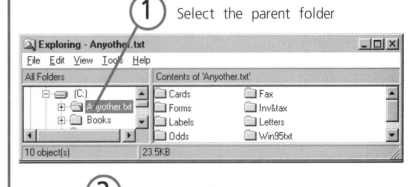

Select the parent folder

Open the **File** menu and point to **New**

Select Folder

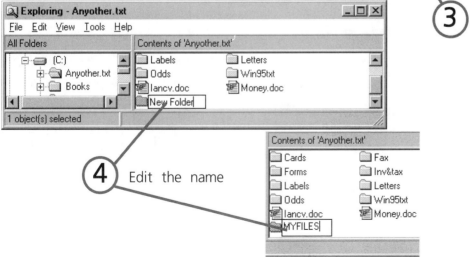

Edit the name

Directory deletion

Deleting a directory is easy using Windows 3.1 – but you need to be careful. All you need to do is to click on the directory and then press [Delete]. Unless you use Confirmation, all of the files and sub-directories will be deleted.

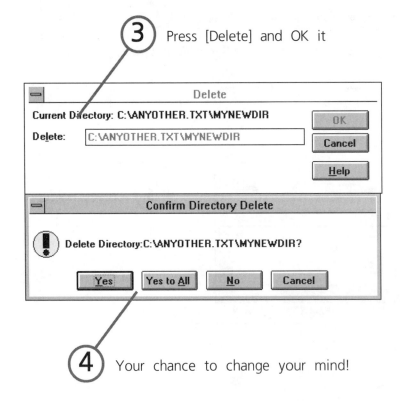

② Check Directory Delete confirmation

Confirmation

Confirm On
- ☐ File Delete
- ☒ Directory Delete
- ☒ File Replace
- ☐ Mouse Action
- ☐ Disk Commands

OK
Cancel
Help

③ Press [Delete] and OK it

Delete

Current Directory: C:\ANYOTHER.TXT\MYNEWDIR

Delete: C:\ANYOTHER.TXT\MYNEWDIR

OK
Cancel
Help

Confirm Directory Delete

⚠ Delete Directory:C:\ANYOTHER.TXT\MYNEWDIR?

Yes   Yes to All   No   Cancel

④ Your chance to change your mind!

❑ Windows 3.1

1 Run **File Manager**, open the **Options** menu, and select **Confirmation**.

2 Make sure that the **Confirm on Directory Delete** item is crossed.

3 When you select a directory and press **[Delete]** you have a chance to change your mind after the OK dialog box.

4 In the Confirm dialog box **Yes** deletes the named directory. **Yes to All** deletes all the subdirectories without the need to confirm.

Take note

If you do not use **Confirm on Delete Directory**, you might someday manage to delete almost everything on your hard drive.

Basic steps

1 To delete a directory, click on its name and then press **[Delete]**.

  You will see the Confirmation notice.

2 Click on **Yes**.

❑ **Recovering files**

  'Deleted' files are stored in the bin.

3 Click on the **Recycled** icon, or **Recycle Bin**.

4 You will see the 'deleted' files. Click on any you want to recover.

5 Use **File – Restore** to recover the files.

❑ You can use **File – Empty Recycle Bin** to make the deletion permanent.

Use this for permament deletion.

Deleting in Windows 95

When you delete a folder or set of folders in Windows-95 you do not delete the files in the folders. Instead, you send them to the Recycle Bin. The folder may have gone for good, but the files have not, because you can recover them from the bin until such time as you empty it.

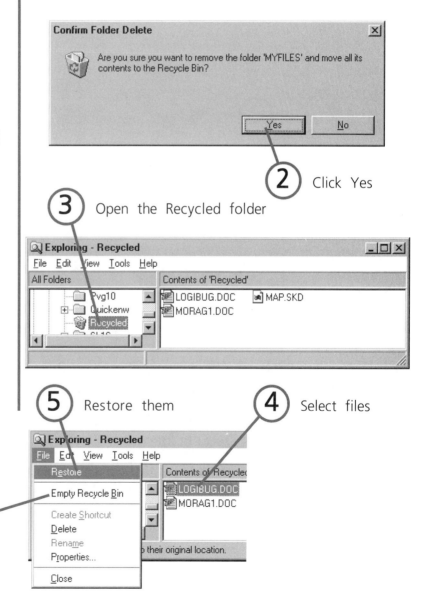

File Manager display

The normal way that the machine arranges directories and files is in the order that they are saved to the disk. This is not convenient, and Windows makes it particularly easy to alter this arrangement.

In a normal sorted list, all the directory names will appear, sorted in order, before any filenames appear.

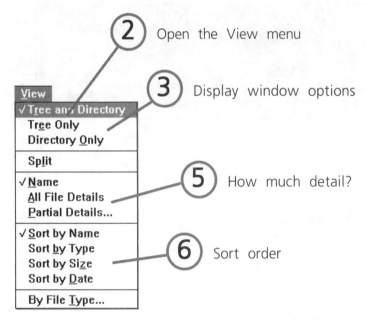

(2) Open the View menu

(3) Display window options

(5) How much detail?

(6) Sort order

Sort by Name will list your files in alphabetical order of the filename, starting with A and ending with Z.

Sort by Type arranges them in order of extension letters, so that BAT comes ahead of ZIP.

Sort by Size places the largest files at the top, smallest at the bottom of the list.

Sort by date puts your most recently edited or created files first, old ones last.

1 Run **File Manager**.

2 Click on the **View** menu to see the main options.

3 In the first section, choose whether to see **Tree and Directory** (the default), **Tree only** or **Directory only**.

4 You can opt to see **Name** only, or more **Details** of the files.

5 You can then opt to Sort by **Name**, **Type** (extension letters), **Size** or **Date**.

Tip

A sort by date is a very useful way of finding old files that you might want to delete.

Basic steps

☐ **File Manager**

1 *Either* Click on **Split** in the **View** menu. You will see the dividing line emphasised, with a two-way arrow.

Or place the pointer on the dividing line until you see the arrows, then drag it.

2 Drag the line where you want it and click to anchor it.

☐ **Explorer**

1 Move the pointer over the dividing line of the **Explorer** window and drag it to left or right.

Take note

You need to move the dividing line more often when you use Explorer, because of the way that the width of the left-hand column changes.

The Split

There is another useful item in the menu, labelled as **Split**. When you click on this one in File Manager, you can click on the line that divides the sections and move it where you want.

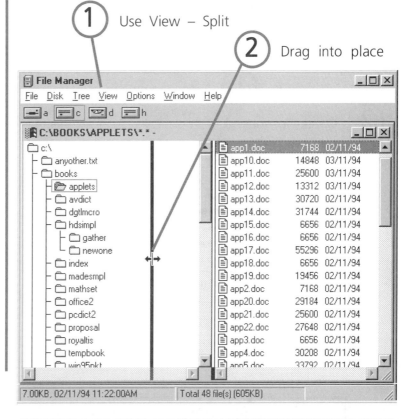

① Use View – Split

② Drag into place

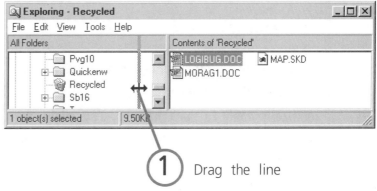

① Drag the line

Sorting by Type

The File Manager View menu also contains the **By File Type** item, which leads to a dialog box. This allows you to use a wildcard specification, or to indicate specific types of entries. You can also make a more general option about the type of files that you show.

These options will remain in force until you change them

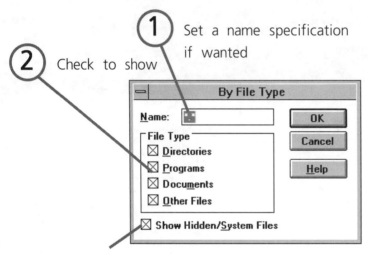

① Set a name specification if wanted

② Check to show

Keep these hidden to stop accidental deletion

1 Set the **Name** if you only want to show particular files, such as *.PCX or *.DOC.

2 Click the **File Type** boxes to show (checked) or hide (clear):

   Directories

   Programs (files with COM or EXE extensions.

   Documents (files with extensions such as DOC or TXT)

   Other files – not Programs or Documents

3 Click OK.

❑ **Hidden/System** files are usually files that are essential to the working of the computer. Deleting them would make the system unusable, so it's best if they remain unseen.

Take note

If you use two File Manager displays on one Window, the View options you make for one file set do not automatically apply to the other set. You might, for example, show only directories in one set and only PCX files in the other.

36

Basic steps

Explorer Sorting

1 Click on **View**, then move the pointer to **Arrange Icons**.

2 Click on the type of sort you want, or leave the setting at **Auto Arrange**.

❑ **To hide file types:**

3 Click on the **Options** item in **View**. Click on the option you want to use.

Windows-95 Explorer uses the Arrange Icons item on its View menu for sorting. You can, however, leave this set at Auto Arrange (by name) unless you need some other form of sorting.

If you want to hide some file types, click on View Options. You can choose whether or not to show files of these types, and you can also opt whether or not to show DOS path information and DOS extensions along with file names.

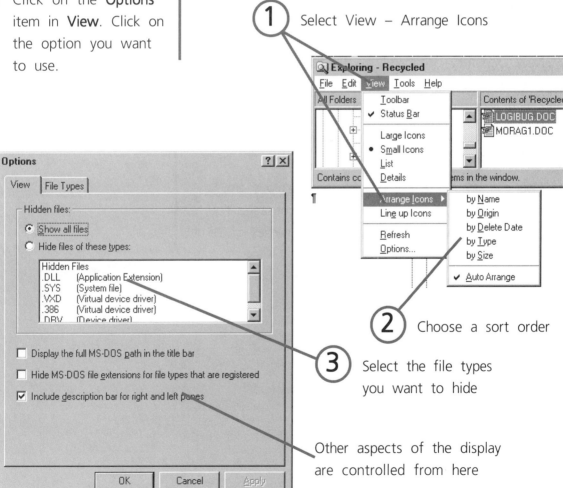

① Select View – Arrange Icons

② Choose a sort order

③ Select the file types you want to hide

Other aspects of the display are controlled from here

Summary

❑ You move to a Windows directory by clicking on it. If a [+] box appears next to a directory name, click on it to show the sub-directories.

❑ Windows 95 calls directories **folders**, and Explorer is the preferred way of working with folders.

❑ You may need to specify a **path** for some Windows programs. The easiest way to do this is to use the **Browse** key that appears when you need to specify a path. Windows 95 also provides a button for creating a new folder when you might need one.

❑ In File Manager, you make a directory by using the **New Directory** command of the File menu. You have to type a name. Explorer creates a directory called **New Folder** which you can rename.

❑ You can **delete a directory** by clicking on its name and pressing [Delete].

❑ You can ensure that your directory displays are **sorted into order** of name, type, size or age. You can also opt to reveal or conceal the names of some types of file.

4 Backups

Simple backup

Making backups of your files on the hard drive is not just a good idea, it is utterly essential. Some day the hard drive will fail, but between now and then you will probably manage to delete a large number of files that you would prefer to keep. We'll look later at the way that files can be recovered after deletion, but don't rely on it.

The simplest form of backup is the easiest – just make a copy of every file that you create as soon as you save it on the hard drive.

1 After you save a new file on the hard drive, run **File Manager**.

2 Find the new file, click on it and drag it to the **A:** drive icon.

3 Using Windows 95 **Explorer**, drag the file to the **A:** (3° Floppy) icon in the list on the left-hand side

4 Windows Explorer can also be used if there are directories on the floppy.

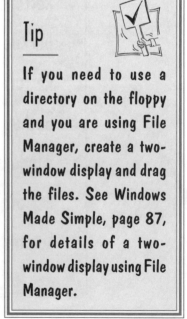

Tip

If you need to use a directory on the floppy and you are using File Manager, create a two-window display and drag the files. See Windows Made Simple, page 87, for details of a two-window display using File Manager.

① Select the file

② Drag to the A: icon

③ Drag to the Floppy icon

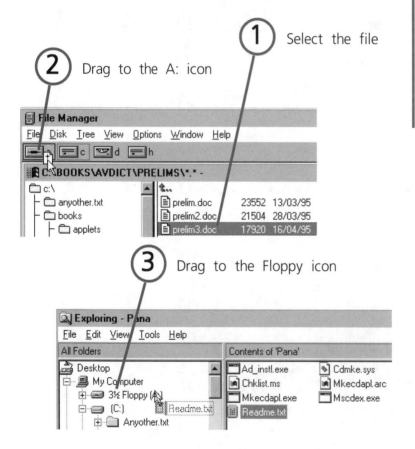

Program utilities

1 While **Word** is running, click on **Tools** then **Macro**.

2 Type as the **Macro name** AUTOCLOSE.

3 Click on **Create**

You will see a blank form with the lines *SUB MAIN* and *End Sub* already in place.

4 Type the other lines in between and close the file to record it as AUTOCLOSE.

5 This will run when any file is closed, asking you if you want a backup and backing the file to a floppy.

Some programs will themselves provide for making automatic backups, but these usually require you to have some programming skills to create *macros*.

Don't let this requirement phase you, as all that is usually needed is the ability to modify an example; you might even see something in print that suits you perfectly.

The example shown on the following page is from Microsoft Word. It uses a macro created using Word and saved as AUTOEXIT. It will copy to a floppy any file that has been saved to the hard drive and then closed.

(2) Type a name

(3) Click Create

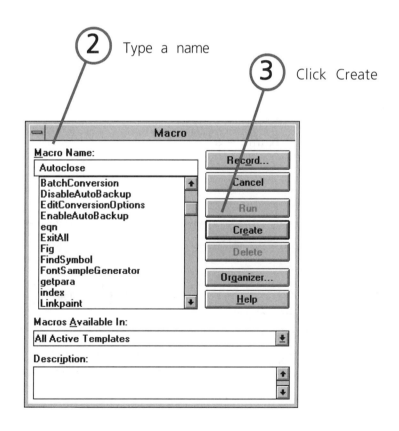

Tip

Use a DriveSpaced floppy for your backups. (see Section 7)

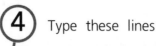 Type these lines

Comments

☐ This might look fear-some, but it's all ready to type and use, you don't need to adapt it if you use Word versions 2 or 6.

☐ Most of the complications arise because the program has to find the filename, separating it from the drive and directory names.

☐ The programming language is called WordBasic, and it is used extensively for Microsoft programs to allow you to tailor the programs to your own needs.

Autoclose example

```
Sub MAIN
a$ = FileName$(1)
If Right$(a$, 3) <> "DOC" Then Goto getout
n = MsgBox("Save to A:\?", "Backup Option", 36)
If n = 0 Then Goto getout
j = Len(a$)
For n = j To 1 Step - 1
  If Mid$(a$, n, 1) = "\" Then
    k = j - n
    n = 1
  End If
Next
a$ = Right$(a$, k)
a$ = "A:\" + a$
FileSaveAs .Name = a$
getout:
End Sub
```

Here's what you see on screen when you close a file. Click on **Yes** to save the file to a floppy.

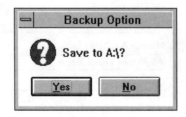

Basic steps

MWBackup

1 Double-click on the **MWBACKUP** icon. The first time you use it, you will be offered a **Configuration** option. Accept it.

2 You will see a notice about using the A: drive for a trial backup. Place a blank floppy in the drive and click on **Start** when you are ready.

3 You must not Run anything that would use the floppy drive during the test.

4 Watch the progress report and change disks when prompted.

Take note

If you use **DriveSpace** on your floppy disks you will need to prepare floppies that are not **DriveSpaced**.

The main Windows 3.1 backup system is MWBACKUP. If you cannot find any trace of this you will have to install it. The files for MWBACKUP are not included with Windows 3.1, they are on the MS-DOS 6.22 distribution disks.

Windows 95 uses an updated system, see later.

MWBACKUP will not work right away, because it needs to be configured for your computer. This involves making a one-off trial backup and reading it back. You will need to have some floppy disks formatted ready for use.

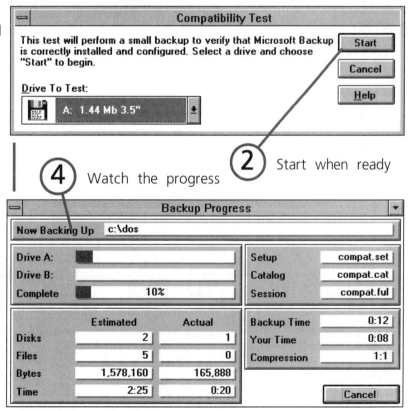

What this test does is to backup some test files onto a couple of floppies, and test that they can be read back with perfect accuracy. You will be asked to re-insert the disks in order.

Comparing

The second phase is reading back the files from the floppy disks to compare them with the originals.

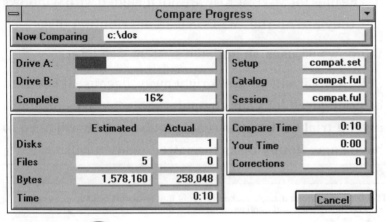

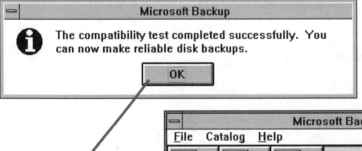
Watch for the prompts

Success!

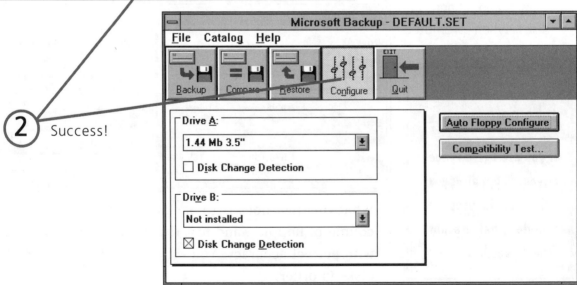

1 When prompted, insert the first backup floppy in the drive and click **OK**. and again with the second.

2 When it is finished, you will see a notice that the system is OK for using BACKUP. At the main screen, the **Configure** icon will be highlighted.

❑ You will be told if anything has gone wrong. Do not use MWBACKUP until a compatibility test has reported success.

Basic steps

1 Click on the **Backup** icon.

2 You will see the panel change so that you can select the hard drive to **Backup from** and the floppy drive to **Backup to**.

3 Click on the **Select Files** button. There will be a pause while your directories are checked. The display is like that of File Manager. Select a directory and files (more than one set if you like).

BACKUP is very flexible, and you can easily get lost in its complications. We'll concentrate on backing up data files in a single directory, setting BACKUP so that only files that have been changed or created are backed up.

① Click Backup

② Pick your disks

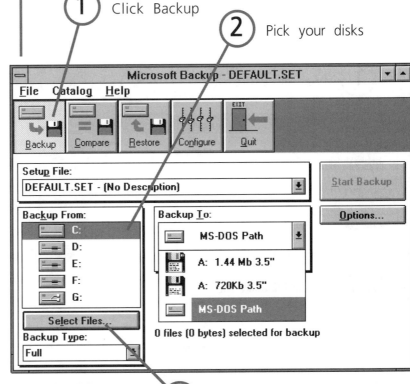

Click the right mouse button or [Shift] and left button to select a filename.

③ Select the files

De-select in same way. A filename that has once been selected appears in red even when deselected.

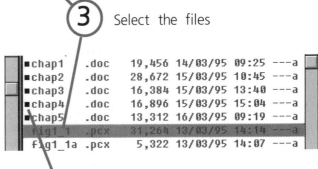

Square dots appear against selected files.

Autoselection

You can select a set of files by dragging the mouse with the right mouse button held down, or giving a wildcard expression in the Include/Exclude dialog box. This can be done ONLY if you first clear all selections by dragging the mouse with both buttons held down. This takes effect only on the next backup when the Setup file (see later) is loaded.

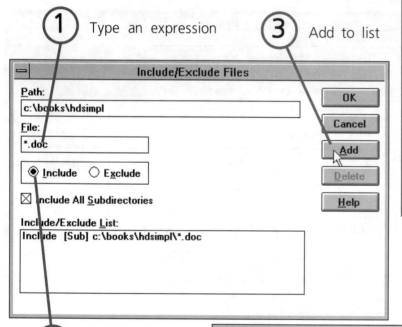

1 Type an expression   **3** Add to list

4 Set to Include or Exclude

Click on **Legend** (main Window) to see this explanation of icons.

1 Click on 🗗 Include at the foot of the Backup window.

2 This opens the **Include /Exclude** dialog box, and you can type the wildcard expression, e.g. *.DOC. The In- clude button is se- lected by default.

3 Click on **Add** to add this selection.

4 You can add other file types, Include or Exclude, and change directory as required.

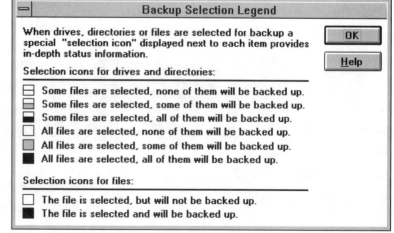

Basic steps

Setting Options and starting

1 Click on the **Options** button.

2 Check that **Compress** is turned on. Set other options as required and click **OK**.

3 Click the Start Backup button.

❑ You will see a report on the backup. The time needed can be very short – 3 seconds for the example of five files totalling 94 Kb

After you have selected files and returned to the main window, set your Options before starting the Backup. Opt to compress the files, otherwise large backups will need very many floppies. (Compression can be as much as 4:1.) The checked options shown here are worth retaining, and you might want to select some others.

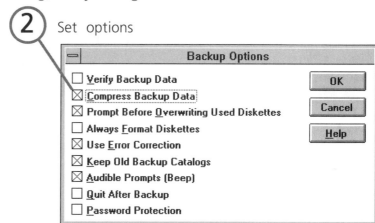

② Set options

Backup Options

☐ <u>V</u>erify Backup Data
☒ <u>C</u>ompress Backup Data
☒ Prompt Before <u>O</u>verwriting Used Diskettes
☐ Always <u>F</u>ormat Diskettes
☒ Use <u>E</u>rror Correction
☒ <u>K</u>eep Old Backup Catalogs
☒ <u>A</u>udible Prompts (Beep)
☐ <u>Q</u>uit After Backup
☐ <u>P</u>assword Protection

[OK] [Cancel] [Help]

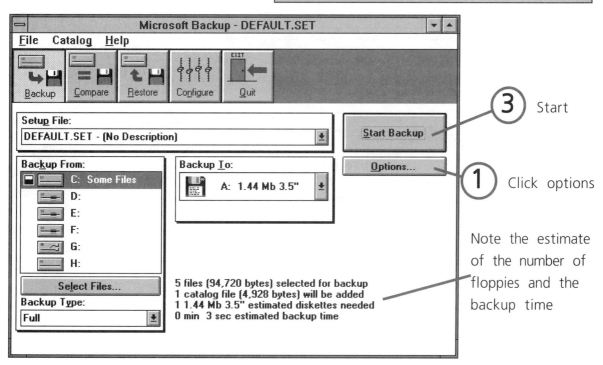

③ Start

① Click options

Note the estimate of the number of floppies and the backup time

Saving configuration

One of the valuable features of MWBACKUP is that you can retain a set of options in the form of a file.

For example, if you chose to backup all *.DOC files in a directory called C:\BOOKS\HDSIMPL, with compression. You can make this your new default set, or save them as a new SETUP file, with the SET extension.

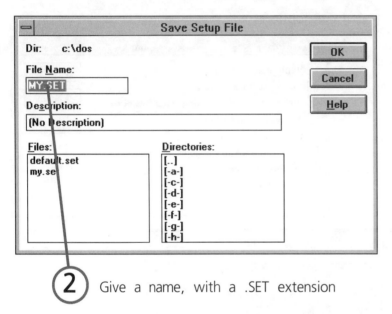

Give a name, with a .SET extension

1 Open the **File** menu and select **Save Setup** to save your Include/ Exclude options as DEFAULT.SET. You next use Backup there is no need to select files again if you want the same selection.

2 If you retain the original DEFAULT.SET, use **File – Save Setup As** and supply a filename for this setup.

3 When you next want to backup the same selection, use **File – Open Setup** to load in your own setup file.

Select a setup file

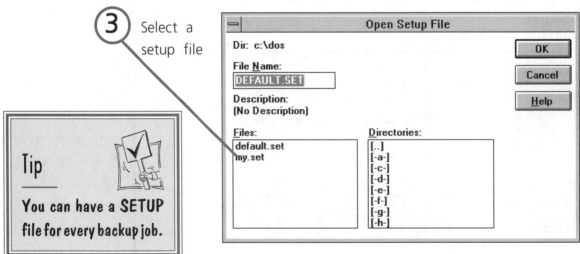

> **Tip**
>
> You can have a SETUP file for every backup job.

48

Basic steps

1 Click on the **Restore** icon.

2 Select whether to **Restore to** the original directory or to other drives or directories.

3 Use the **Select Files** button to see the files in the backup, and select the ones you want to restore.

4 Set any **Options** as required.

5 Click on **Start Restore**.

Restoring files

There would be no point in using MWBACKUP if you could not recover the files after of a disk disaster. Though the configuration tests the system, the real test is to delete some files and check that you can recover them. This is also done through MWBACKUP.

Set these if you are worried about what a Resore may do to your disk structure

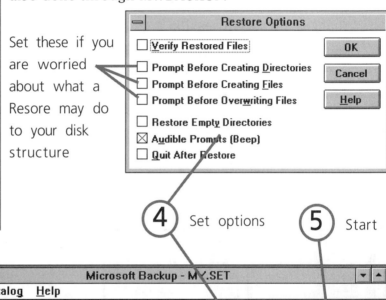

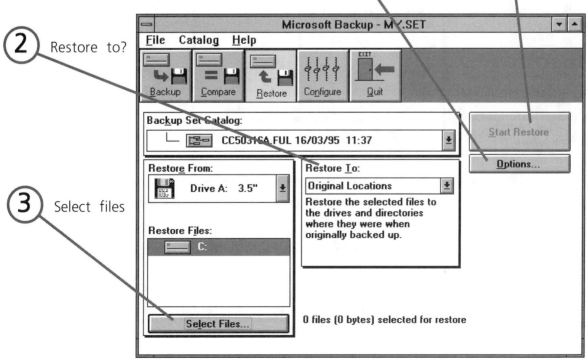

(2) Restore to?

(3) Select files

(4) Set options

(5) Start

Backup routines

There are three types of Backup that MWBACKUP can carry out, called Full, Incremental and Differential.

- Start with a Full backup for files that have never been backed up before.
- Use Incremental or Differential to keep track of changes after each session.
- Make a Full backup weekly or monthly, depending on how intensively you create and alter files.

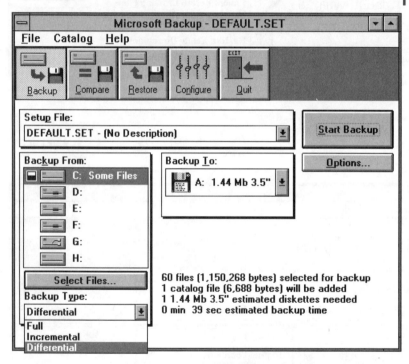

Types

- ❏ **Full** backup will back up all the selected files each time.

- ❏ **Incremental** backup will back up only the files that have changed since the last backup. This is the most useful type, particularly if you edit a set of the same files each working day.

- ❏ **Differential** backup will backup all the files that have changed since the last Full backup, and also files that were saved in any Differential backups.

Take note

Remember that the Include or Exclude wildcard options that you have used will take effect only if you have saved your setup file and quit Backup, then re-started Backup.

Notes

❑ You cannot back up a file that is still open.

❑ You can use Include for files that you have not yet created, particularly if you use the option to include sub-directories. When the files are created, they will be backed up next time you use Backup.

❑ You can select all files in a directory by double-clicking on the directory name. This allows you to use Exclude if you want to exclude some types of files, such as EXE and COM, from a data set.

❑ The more care you take with your SET file, the more useful your backups will be.

Looking further

You can select all the files on your hard drive by double-clicking the C:\ root name. If you select differential backup this is a good way of ensuring that you back up altered files, but a Full backup of your entire hard drive would take a long time and use a large number of disks.

For example, my hard drive currently uses 178 Mbyte, and would need 91 floppies and 76 minutes for backup. This is just an estimate, more might be needed— though if you use compression you will normally need fewer floppies than this report calls for.

This means that Backup using floppies is best used selectively. Because it allows the disk directory structure to be restored as well as the files, it can be very useful if a portion of a disk becomes wiped or unusable.

If you need the peace of mind that a full backup of a complete hard drive brings, the best option is a tape streamer, using a drive such as the well-known Colorado. These are now comparatively inexpensive, and will back up a 250 Mbyte hard drive to one small tape cartridge. Once you have made a full backup in this way, you can use floppies for your incremental backups.

Take note

You must keep all incremental backups until you make another full backup.

Restoring old files

MWBACKUP is the system that you should use if you have up to date copies of MS-DOS and Windows, but you may have some floppies that were created using the old DOS Backup utility in MS-DOS versions earlier than 6.0. You cannot use MWBACKUP or MSBACKUP (see next page) to read such floppies.

In addition, you need to use different methods to restore files from floppies that were backed up from MS-DOS versions 6.0 and 6.2. These versions used MWBACKUP and MSBACKUP, but with a different compression method used for the files.

Using RESTORE

RESTORE must be run from DOS. The command line must contain the drive letter for the floppy, and the drive and directory to which the file must be restored.

Unlike MWBACKUP, you cannot use RESTORE to restore a file to a different directory, though you can use a different drive.

Example:

    RESTORE A: C:\WORDS\MYDOC.TXT

will restore the file called MYDOC.TXT into its directory (WORDS) on the C: drive, using a floppy in the A: drive.

You can use

    RESTORE A: C:*.* /S

to restore all files from the floppy to the hard drive. This restoration will include all of the directories because it uses the /S option.

- ❏ You can use option letters following a RESTORE line, with a forward slash used to separate these options from the main command and from each other.

- /S will ensure that sub-directories are restored. This is the most useful of the options.

- /N will restore only the files that are no longer on the hard drive.

- /D will display the names of files that are available to be restored, but without actually carrying out the restore action.

- ❏ You can also opt to restore only these files that were last changed on, before or after some specified time or date.

Considerations

❏ Your data cannot be insured. Backup is your only safeguard.

❏ Any business that suffers total loss of data usually fails very quickly.

❏ The hazards are theft of your computer, theft of your floppies, breakdown, and fire

❏ Even floppy backups, kept in a different place (next door, the bank, even your pocket) provide some safeguard.

❏ Digital tapes are compact and hold very much more data. The smaller sizes are ideal for all but large-scale users of computers.

If your work with the computer is important, and especially if you earn a living from it, you should consider a tape or removable hard drive backup system.

Tape streamers

Systems such as the well-known Colorado Jumbo, and Iomega, are now reasonably priced (about £100 to £200). These can be installed internally like a 3.5" disk drive, or bought as external units (costing more) that plug into a parallel port. These units are ideal for backups in the 100 Mbyte to 800 Mbyte range, and they use tape cartridges that cost about £15.

For larger capacity, you can buy a DAT cartridge system which is much more expensive - about £800 upwards for 8 to 16 Gbyte storage.

Removable hard drives

Another security option is the removable hard drive. This is either an external or internal unit, and the drive portion can be unplugged and put in a bank vault for safe keeping after you have copied all your files to it.

Take note

If you use **DriveSpace** you may not be able to use **Syquest** removable hard drives. The two can conflict on some systems.

Windows 95 Backup

Basic steps

Windows 95 keeps its backup programs in a set called System Tools. This is usually tucked away among the Accessories. When you place the cursor on this name, you should see the individual program names and icons.

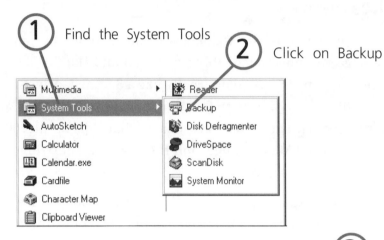

① Find the System Tools

② Click on Backup

1 Click on **Start** and move the pointer through **Programs** and **Accessories** to the **System Tools** set.

2 Select **Backup**.

3 Click ☒ to reject the **Full System Backup** – use it only if you have a tape streamer or 80 or more floppies to spare. Selective backup is usually a better option.

③ Reject the offer

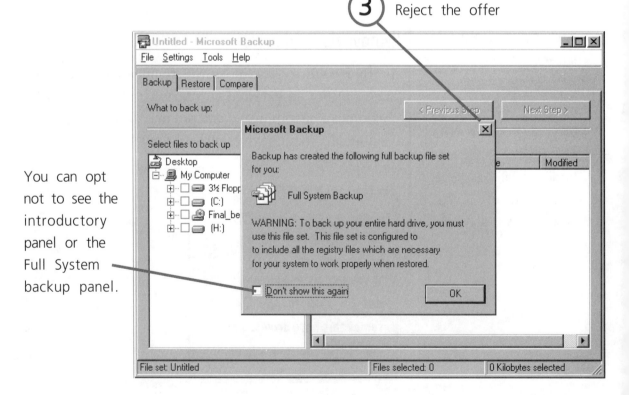

You can opt not to see the introductory panel or the Full System backup panel.

Basic steps

Selective backup

1 Click on the **C:** drive to list its folders.

2 Click on the ☐ by the name to select all of the files in the folder

   Or click on the folder name to open it and select individual files to backup

3 You can delete a tick against a file or folder by clicking again.

4 When you have finished ticking files and folders, click on

   Next Step >

5 Select the destination – **A:** if you use floppies, or a tape drive if you have one.

Backup starts by choosing folders and files. A tick in the small box next to a file or folder name means that it will be backed up.

You can select all the files in a folder by clicking on its box, or open the folder and select files individually.

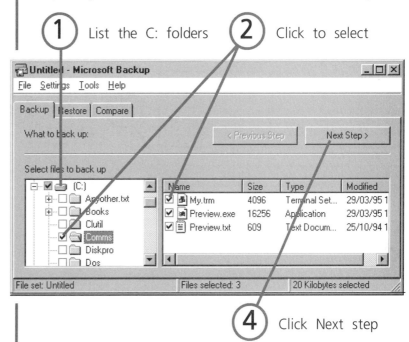

① List the C: folders ② Click to select

④ Click Next step

⑤ Select the destination

Selective Backup

If you have made a selection that you are likely to want to use again, you can save a catalogue file much in the same way as with Windows 3.1.

You can also name your backup file, and you can use a password.

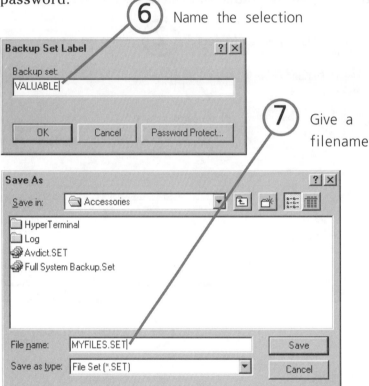

Name the selection

Give a filename

6 When you have selected a drive to save your files to, you can also save your Backup set (catalogue) for use again.

7 Finally, click on **Start Backup**. You will be asked for a filename and given the option of adding a password.

Take note

If the floppy already contains files you will be asked if you want to erase them, or use a different floppy.

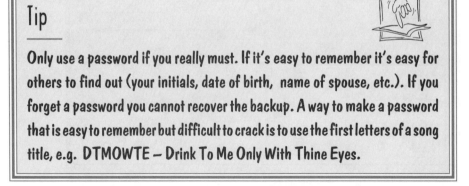

Tip

Only use a password if you really must. If it's easy to remember it's easy for others to find out (your initials, date of birth, name of spouse, etc.). If you forget a password you cannot recover the backup. A way to make a password that is easy to remember but difficult to crack is to use the first letters of a song title, e.g. DTMOWTE – Drink To Me Only With Thine Eyes.

Basic steps

Restore and Compare

1. Open the **Restore** tab.

2. Specify the drive that contains the backup.

3. Click [Next Step >].
   When the drive starts, the name of the destination folder will appear.

4. Click on this to show the file name(s).

5. Click [Start Restore] to restore the files

❑ The **Compare** action is used in exactly the same way, but it delivers a report on any differences between files.

Backup contains tabs marked **Backup**, **Restore** and **Compare** and all three actions are run from the one panel.

You can **Restore** by specifying the backup name in the drive that you used for the backup. You can restore to the same folders or re-create the original folders.

The **Compare** action will compare the contents of the backup with the current contents of your folders to find if there is any discrepancy. Do this to check the files before backing up.

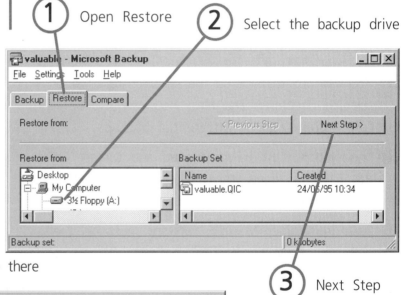

① Open Restore

② Select the backup drive

③ Next Step

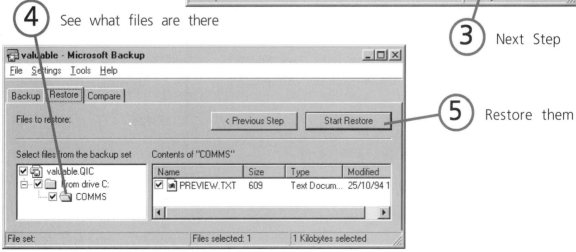

④ See what files are there

⑤ Restore them

Summary

❏ You must **always back up data files**, and the simplest method is to copy such files to a floppy immediately after saving to the hard drive.

❏ Some programs provide for writing commands in a Macro language so that you can write **automatic backup systems** for the data that these programs create.

❏ You can **use a DriveSpaced floppy** for backup, so that fewer floppies are needed.

❏ The main backup system for Windows is **MWBACKUP**. This allows you to use file compression so that it can be economical on floppies.

❏ You can opt to back up the whole hard drive or selected directories and files. You can also opt for **Full**, **Incremental** or **Differential** backups.

❏ The system must be **configured and tested**. Once this has been done you can be confident about its ability to hold your data and restore it.

❏ Data from **older MS-DOS versions** must be dealt with separately. For versions before 6.0, you need to use the RESTORE DOS command.

❏ A **tape system** can be useful if you have valuable data to back up. The smaller systems are relative inexpensive.

❏ **Windows 95** contains its own **Backup** system, with options of Backup, Restore and Compare.

5 Speed and efficiency

Hardware and speed

The hardware of a hard drive determines its ultimate speed, and there's not a lot you can do other than get out the screwdriver and make changes. We'll look at that later.

If your computer is slow when it comes to hard drive actions you might be thinking of replacing the whole computer. If so, you need to know what to look for. You'll probably be aiming at a 486 or Pentium type of machine, and the faster the clock speed you can afford the better. Think in terms of 50 MHz, 75 MHz or even 100 MHz.

You will also need to ensure that your new computer has a local bus for its disk drive. The speed difference can be impressive, and the local bus is also used for the graphics card so that your displays operate faster.

Take note

You might think that smaller-capacity hard drives would be faster. There is no relationship between capacity and speed, so go for the largest and fastest you can afford. In six months you'll want more space and more speed.

A hard drive with a built-in cache memory is faster than a comparable drive without a cache.

Points

1 Use as fast a drive as possible. The speed of a drive is measured in terms of access time in milliseconds, and the lower this figure the faster the drive. Times of 12 - 15ms are typical.

2 Use a hard drive that is connected by way of a **local bus**. This ensure much faster running than you can get when the drive is connected through the ordinary expansion slots of the computer.

3 If you use Windows, make sure that you are using the most recent version. By the time you read this Windows 95 will be available, but if your memory size is less than 8 Mbyte you might be better off with Windows 3.1.

Points

1 Make sure you have enough memory. It is difficult to have too much memory, particularly for Windows, and if you are using modern memory-hungry programs like Word-6 or Excel even 8 Mbyte is not at all a large amount of memory.

2 Quite apart from using some memory as cache, having enough memory avoids the need to keep using the hard drive when you swap Windows programs around.

3 Make sure that the SMARTDRV cache program is installed in your AUTOEXEC.BAT file. See next page for details.

Using cache memory

We can't always buy a new machine when we find we need more speed and/or more capacity. Sometimes a computer can be upgraded (see the book *Build Your Own PC*, from Butterworth-Heinemann), but you might not realise just how much can be achieved by using software.

The most important software from the point of view of hard drive speeds is cache software. A cache is a piece of memory used to hold data that has been read from the disk or is to be written to the disk. The principle is that the cache memory is read or written when the computer does not use the disk for anything else, and the data in the cache is used in preference to data on the disk as far as possible. Since memory is much faster than disk, this can speed up actions quite impressively.

One snag as far as this is concerned is that the cache takes up memory, often 1 Mbyte or more. You can't have too much memory.

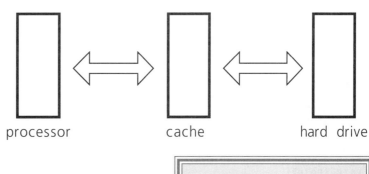

processor   cache   hard drive

Take note

If you use Windows 95, you don't need **SMARTDRV**.

Smartdrive

Smartdrive, in the form of the file SMARTDRV.EXE, is the Microsoft cache program that can speed up hard drive actions. If you use multimedia, it will also speed up the CD-ROM actions provided that Smartdrive is installed correctly.

1 Start **Notepad**.

2 Click on **File – Open** and set the filename to ***.BAT**. Change the Directory to **C:**

3 Double-click on **AUTOEXEC.BAT**.

4 Somewhere in the file you should find a line containing: **SMARTDRV.EXE**

Here, **LH** means that this file has been Loaded into High memory. The important point is that it is almost the last line. The last might be WIN to start Windows.

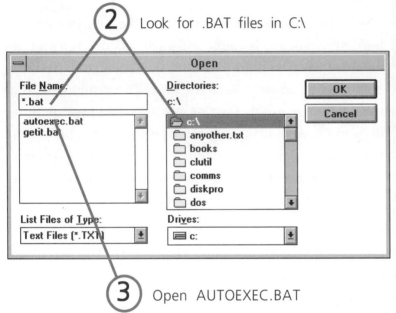

② Look for .BAT files in C:\

③ Open AUTOEXEC.BAT

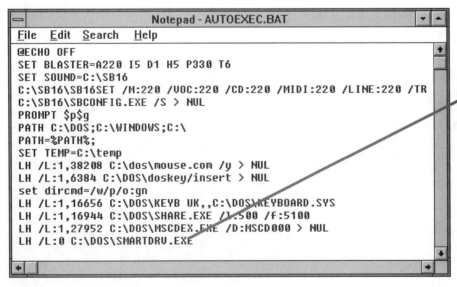

④ Check that SMARTDRV is there

Notes

1 If SmartDrive is not present in your AUTOEXEC.BAT, look for SMARTDRV.EXE in the C:\DOS directory. If it is not present, you will need to install it manually from the MS-DOS floppy – see *the Pocket Book of MS-DOS* for details.

2 After SmartDrive is installed, you can reboot and use MEMMAKER to position it so as to release more memory for use by other programs.

3 To see how SmartDrive is used, switch to MS-DOS and make the DOS directory current. Type the command:

SMARTDRV /S

to see the display of memory and cache use.

Using SmartDrive

The simple SMARTDRV.EXE line in AUTOEXEC.BAT will ensure that the cache is installed, but it doesn't tell you much about it. In fact, using SmartDrive like this will ensure that it is well-adapted to the resources of your computer, and you should not attempt to alter the settings until you have more experience.

```
Cache size:  2,097,152 bytes
Cache size while running Windows:   2,097,152 bytes

                Disk Caching Status
drive    read cache    write cache    buffering
----------------------------------------------------
  A:*       yes            no            no
  B:        yes            no            no
  C:*       yes            yes           no
  D:        yes            no            no
  E:        yes            no            no
  F:        yes            no            no
  G:        yes            no            no
  H:        yes            yes           no
  K:        yes            no            no

* Compressed drive cached via host drive.
```

Take note

SmartDrive, in this example, is using about 2 Mbyte from a total memory of 8 Mbyte. It will use less if you have a smaller memory size.

Only the hard drive is cached for both reading and writing, and you are reminded that you should not switch off the computer until you see the C:> sign return to indicate that the cache contents have been written to the hard drive.

Read and write cache

SMARTDRV will always cache reading actions. That means that it will read from the disk and keep a store of the bytes that it finds. It can then supply these quickly to your computer when they are needed.

SMARTDRV can also cache writing actions. If it is used this way, when you save a file the data is stored in the cache, and is passed to the hard drive later, usually when there is no other call upon the hard drive.

There is a risk involved here. If you save all your files and switch off the computer, the files will be in the cache, not on the hard drive, and they will be lost forever. You must always wait for the C:> prompt to appear if you use cache writing with Windows 3.1.

Windows 95 puts a notice on the screen telling you when it is safe to switch off.

Windows 95 uses its own cache system that works on read and write and you do not need to do anything unless you want to alter the cache size for a CD-ROM.

See the next page for details.

Points

❑ If your AUTOEXEC.BAT file contains the line:

SMARTDRV

then the cache is for both writing and reading.

❑ If you are worried about **write caching**, alter the line to read:

SMARTDRV C

which will make the action work on reading only.

❑ There is an option referred to as **double-buffering**. Ignore this unless an expert tells you that it is necessary.

Basic steps

1 Click the **Start** button and move to **Settings**. Click on **Control Panel**.

2 Double-click the **File System** icon System

3 Click the tab marked **Performance** and then the **File System** button. Make sure that the correct speed of your CD-ROM drive appears.

4 Click on the Slider for Supplemental Cache Size and drag it to a larger size (noted in the text below)

Caching in Windows 95

The cache system that is used in Windows 95 is quite different and is referred to as VCACHE. There is also a supplementary cache called CDFS that is used for CD-ROM drives.

You should not normally need to make any alteration to the settings of these programs, and certainly not without taking advice. The steps that appear on this page are for information – do not feel that you must carry them out.

You might want to check the CD-ROM cache, if you use CD-ROM. You should not disable write-behind caching unless you think it might cause problems, and only if you know what you are doing. For that reason, there are no instructions here..

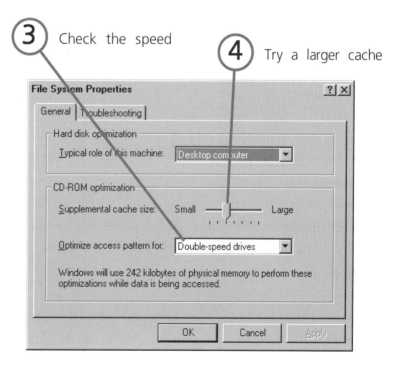

③ Check the speed

④ Try a larger cache

Drive housekeeping

A hard drive performs most efficiently when it is new and you have just loaded in all the programs and data.

From then on, it's all down hill, because you are likely to delete files and add new ones. This eventually leaves the drive in an Emmenthal state – full of holes. Like this, it takes longer to get data because the bytes of your files are scattered around the drive.

You can get around this by using disk utilities that will defragment the disk, ensuring that all the bytes of each file are gathered together.

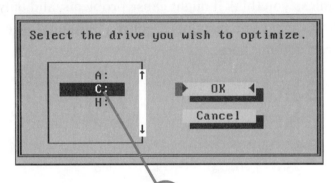

The H drive shown here arises from the use of DriveSpace, see later.

 Select a drive

Take note

You must never use a disk defragmenter while you are running Windows 3.1. This includes using the MS-DOS Prompt. Windows must be shut down. You can, however, use the Defragmenter of Windows 95 without leaving Windows – see later.

Basic steps

❑ **Windows 3.1/DOS**

1 Quit Windows, and make the DOS directory current.

2 Type the command **DEFRAG**.

3 Select the drive to defragment. The default is C: – you would not need to defragment a floppy.

4 The file storage is analysed. Names of directories will appear while this is going on.

5 The analysis is shown as a pattern of small rectangles. The more broken-up this is, the more your hard drive needs this attention.

6 Display the **Legends** to see what the symbols tell you about the amount of the disk that is used and what it is used for.

I keep my hard drive defragmented, as the illustration shows.

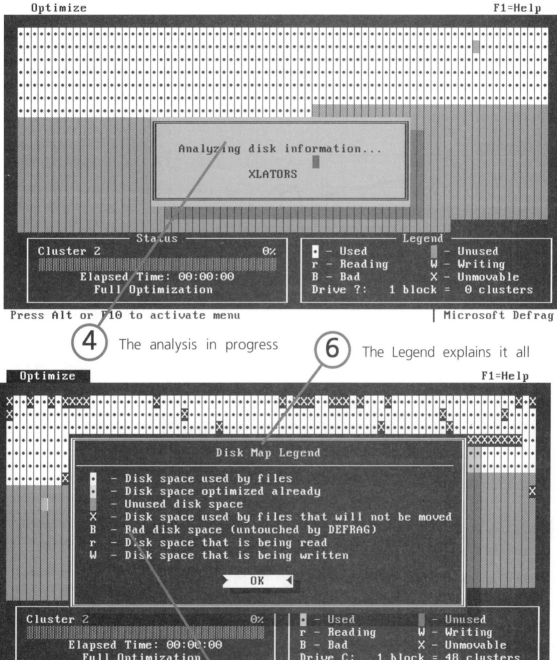

Analyzing disk information...

XLATORS

```
──────────── Status ────────────        ──────────── Legend ────────────
Cluster 2                      0%        • – Used           ▓ – Unused
                                         r – Reading        W – Writing
        Elapsed Time: 00:00:00           B – Bad            X – Unmovable
        Full Optimization                Drive ?:    1 block =   0 clusters
```

Press Alt or F10 to activate menu | Microsoft Defrag

④ The analysis in progress   ⑥ The Legend explains it all

Optimize   F1=Help

```
──────────────── Disk Map Legend ────────────────
  •  – Disk space used by files
  •  – Disk space optimized already
     – Unused disk space
  X  – Disk space used by files that will not be moved
  B  – Bad disk space (untouched by DEFRAG)
  r  – Disk space that is being read
  W  – Disk space that is being written

              ►    OK    ◄
```

```
──────────── ──────────────        ──────────── Legend ────────────
Cluster 2                      0%        • – Used           ▓ – Unused
                                         r – Reading        W – Writing
        Elapsed Time: 00:00:00           B – Bad            X – Unmovable
        Full Optimization                Drive C:    1 block =  48 clusters
```

Show the map symbols definitions | Microsoft Defrag

Don't worry if your drive has portions that are
labelled as BAD. These will not be used.

67

Final touches

The final stage is to defragment your files, so that each is stored in a continuous run on the disk.

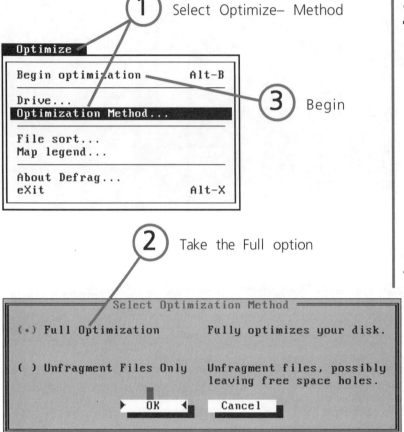

① Select Optimize– Method

Optimize

Begin optimization	Alt-B
Drive...	
Optimization Method...	
File sort...	
Map legend...	
About Defrag...	
eXit	Alt-X

③ Begin

② Take the Full option

Select Optimization Method

(•) Full Optimization   Fully optimizes your disk.

( ) Unfragment Files Only   Unfragment files, possibly
                            leaving free space holes.

▶ OK ◀   Cancel

1 Open the **Optimize** menu and select **Optimization method**

2 From the panel, select the type of optimisation. You would normally want to perform a **Full Optimization**. The alternative of **Unfragment Files Only** will speed up disk actions but not to the same extent.

3 Click **Begin optimiz-ation** to start it off.

If you get a report about the condition of your drive, with comments about loose clusters, this is a sign that some files have become damaged. The report will suggest what to do (see later regarding SCANDISK and CHKDISK) and one option is to gather the fragments into a file. This is useful, but the file may not be unless all the fragments were of text files.

Take note

Full optimisation of a hard drive that has been extensively used can take an hour or so. Don't start unless you can finish!

4 When defragmentation has been completed, use the **File Sort** option to sort files into order in the directories, setting your criteria in the panel.

5 Always check the state of your disk after you have been deleting files extensively. Section 8 deals with the use of SCANDISK and the older CHKDSK for these purposes.

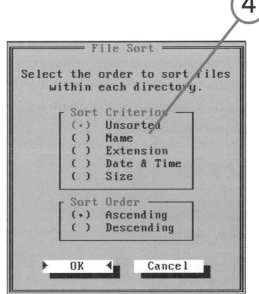

④ Set the criteria and order

The Sort options are no more than you have in Windows, but if you use DOS they can be useful.

Take note

Using DEFRAG is not necessarily useful if you have used DriveSpace on your hard drive. For such drives you need to use the defragmenting utilities in the DriveSpace program set. See Section 7.

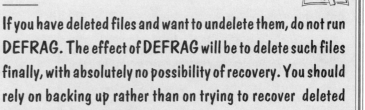

Tip

If you have deleted files and want to undelete them, do not run DEFRAG. The effect of DEFRAG will be to delete such files finally, with absolutely no possibility of recovery. You should rely on backing up rather than on trying to recover deleted files, but no-one is perfect.

The defragmenter

Windows 95 contains its defragmentation program in the same System Tools set as the Backup program. The Defragmenter is run from within Windows-95, with no need to return to DOS. You can even run other programs while the Defragmenter is working, though you should avoid saving or loading files because of the chance that these files are being moved at the time.

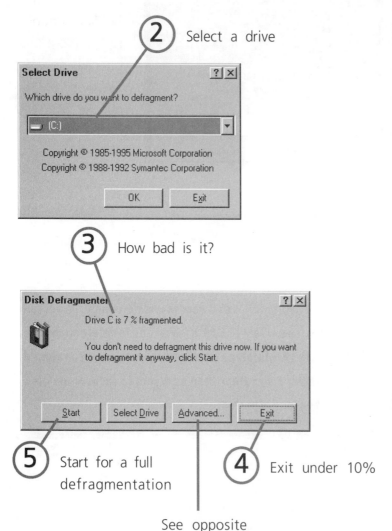

(2) Select a drive

Select Drive ? X

Which drive do you want to defragment?

(C:)

Copyright © 1985-1995 Microsoft Corporation
Copyright © 1988-1992 Symantec Corporation

OK   Exit

(3) How bad is it?

Disk Defragmenter ? X

Drive C is 7 % fragmented.

You don't need to defragment this drive now. If you want to defragment it anyway, click Start.

Start   Select Drive   Advanced...   Exit

(5) Start for a full defragmentation

(4) Exit under 10%

See opposite

1 Click on the **Start** button, and slide the pointer to **Programs**, **Accessories**, and to **System Tools**. Click on **Disk Defragmenter**.

2 Select the drive you want to defragment. The default is C. Click on the **OK** button to go ahead.

3 If you press the **Show Details** button you will be told how fragmented the disk storage is.

4 **Exit** if the disk is only lightly fragmented – anything under 10%.

5 The default is full defragmentation, and since this is what is normally needed, click **Start** if the disk is more than 10% fragmented.

Basic steps

1 Choose **Defragment files only**, to speed up file actions.

2 Choose **Consolidate free space only** if you want to leave the files alone. Note that this can slow down file actions slightly.

3 Always keep the **Check drive for errors** option ticked.

4 Check **Save these options** to ensure that you can use your selected scheme again without clicking the Advanced button.

Advanced options

The Show Details panel contains an Advanced button. This reveals choices for defragmentation. If in doubt, ignore these options and simply use the straightforward system.

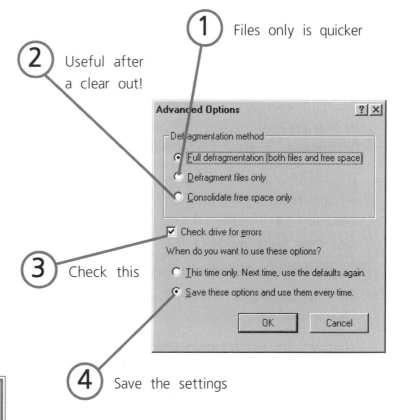

① Files only is quicker

② Useful after a clear out!

③ Check this

④ Save the settings

Tip

This defragmenting program can be used along with a hard drive that uses DriveSpace, see later.

Summary

❑ If your **computer is too slow**, you should think of replacing it with a 486 or Pentium design with a fast clock speed, local bus, and fast hard drive.

❑ A good **cache** for the hard drive helps considerably in speeding up disk access. Make sure that SMARTDRV is installed in the AUTOEXEC.BAT file if you use DOS or Windows 3.1.

❑ As you delete from and add to files in a hard drive, the drive become less efficient because of the need to find portions of files in scattered positions. **Defragment** to make file access much faster.

❑ The **DEFRAG** program can carry out the defragmenting action. It must never be run while Windows 3.1 is active. If you use a DriveSpaced hard drive with Windows 3.1, use the defragmenting program from the DRVSPACE menu.

❑ **Full optimisation** of a hard drive can take a considerable time, an hour or more.

❑ Windows 95 has its own **Disk Defragmenter** which can be used while you are running programs. It also copes automatically with a DriveSpaced drive.

6 DriveSpace

Size is important

No-one ever has enough memory or enough disk space. Each new version of a program has new features that you always wanted, but it needs another few more Mbyte of memory to run and takes up another 10 Mbyte or so on the hard drive.

If you are using a version of MS-DOS between 6.0 and 6.22 you might have the older compression program DoubleSpace. If so, you should convert to DriveSpace as soon as possible because DoubleSpace is no longer supported. If you are not using any form of file compression, DriveSpace does work, it does release more space, and it does not scramble your disk. The compression methods it uses are those used for Backup.

You should have these files in your DOS (or MSDOS) directory. They allow you to install and use DriveSpace on any disk, hard or floppy.

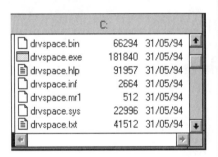

C:		
drvspace.bin	66294	31/05/94
drvspace.exe	181840	31/05/94
drvspace.hlp	91957	31/05/94
drvspace.inf	2664	31/05/94
drvspace.mr1	512	31/05/94
drvspace.sys	22996	31/05/94
drvspace.txt	41512	31/05/94

Tip

Do NOT use DriveSpace if you have a disk drive of the SCSI type, though these are fairly unusual on PC machines.

What can you do?

1 You can release more memory by using MEMMAKER, but that's only dabbling with the problem if you are trying to run Word-6 on a machine with only 4 Mbyte of memory.

2 Hard drive space is cheaper than memory. If your current hard drive is inadequate you can get some more space by purely software methods, using Microsoft DriveSpace.

3 DriveSpace is as close to something for nothing as you will find. It can be used with DOS or Windows but you are more likely to need it if you are using Windows.

4 As always, the methods for Windows 95 are not the same as for Windows 3.1

Basic steps

1 Backup all data files, and make sure you have the distribution disks for all programs. This does not imply any problems with DriveSpace, it's just the normal precautions you would take before changing anything.

2 Leave Windows 3.1.

3 Make the DOS (or MSDOS) directory current and type:

DRVSPACE

4 A Welcome screen appears. Press **[Enter]** to remove this screen.

5 Click the **Express** menu option.

6 Wait. This can take a long time – often more than an hour.

7 When it is done, you will be shown how much space you now have on your hard drive and how much is used.

Installing DriveSpace

The easy option for installing DriveSpace applies if you have one hard drive, letter C:, which is not too full. If that applies, use the **Express Setup**. This will DriveSpace your hard drive with the minimum of fuss and bother. You need use **Custom Setup** only if you want to DriveSpace other hard drives or floppies.

Express Setup will start by checking and defragmenting the drive, and this is one of the factors that causes the process to take so long.

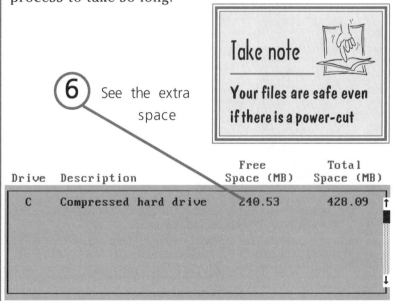

6 See the extra space

Take note

Your files are safe even if there is a power-cut

Drive	Description	Free Space (MB)	Total Space (MB)
C	Compressed hard drive	240.53	428.09

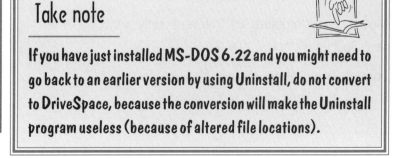

Take note

If you have just installed MS-DOS 6.22 and you might need to go back to an earlier version by using Uninstall, do not convert to DriveSpace, because the conversion will make the Uninstall program useless (because of altered file locations).

Learning more

You might feel that you really don't wish to know this, but it is important to take some time to work it out and take a note of what is displayed. In particular, you need to keep an eye on this information later if you think that space is running out.

Basic steps

1 Run **DRVSPACE** to bring up the main menu.

2 Highlight the drive you are interested in.

3 Open the **Drive** menu and select **Info..** or change a setting.

(2) Select a drive

(3) Find out more

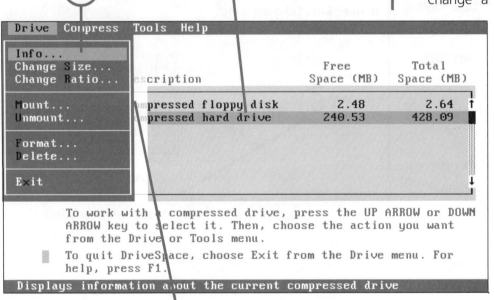

```
 Drive  Compress  Tools  Help

 Info...
 Change Size...                        Free        Total
 Change Ratio...    escription      Space (MB)   Space (MB)

 Mount...            pressed floppy disk     2.48       2.64   ↑
 Unmount...          pressed hard drive    240.53     428.09   ■

 Format...
 Delete...

 Exit                                                          ↓

      To work with a compressed drive, press the UP ARROW or DOWN
      ARROW key to select it. Then, choose the action you want
      from the Drive or Tools menu.
      To quit DriveSpace, choose Exit from the Drive menu. For
      help, press F1.
 Displays information about the current compressed drive
```

Change Size and **Change Ratio** should be left until you have more experience.

Mount and **Unmount** are relevant only with DriveSpaced floppies, see later.

Format and **Delete** should also be left, particularly if only the hard drive is DriveSpaced.

Take note

If you do not want to DriveSpace floppies or add another hard drive you need never use DRVSPACE again.

Notes

❏ When you opt for **Info** in the **Drive** menu, you will see how your files have been compressed, and what estimates have been used.

❏ The fragmentation is also shown in this report.

A typical Info display from DriveSpace

Check the fragmentation level. The higher this is, the more you need to use DEFRAG.

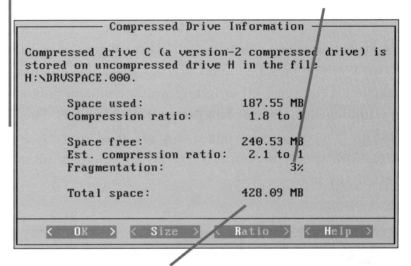

```
┌──────── Compressed Drive Information ────────┐
│ Compressed drive C (a version-2 compressed drive) is │
│ stored on uncompressed drive H in the file │
│ H:\DRVSPACE.000. │
│                                              │
│        Space used:              187.55 MB    │
│        Compression ratio:         1.8 to 1   │
│                                              │
│        Space free:              240.53 MB    │
│        Est. compression ratio:    2.1 to 1   │
│        Fragmentation:                  3%    │
│                                              │
│        Total space:             428.09 MB    │
│                                              │
├──────────────────────────────────────────────┤
│  <   OK   >   <  Size  >   < Ratio >   < Help > │
└──────────────────────────────────────────────┘
```

The total space assumes that the compression ratios are accurate.

Take note

The example shows that the actual compression on the files so far is 1.8, but the remaining space is using an estimate of 2.1. That means the estimate might be optimistic.

Take note

The Space figures are estimates because they assume that files can all be compressed by the same amount. Don't think that because the table shows 40 Mbyte free that you can save 35 Mbyte or so of files.

Text files compress well, as do many graphics files. Some files are already compressed (JPG, ARC, ZIP and so on) and cannot be compressed further.

Using DriveSpace

As far as your are concerned, you continue to use the hard drive C: just as you did before – the difference as far as you are concerned is that it seems to be larger. The DOS DIR command and Windows File Manager will both report the new estimated size, all of which depends on the assumed compression being achieved.

You will now see on any drive list, DOS or Windows, your Drive C which contains most of your files, and a drive labelled H (or some other letter) which contains only a few hidden files, and one labelled as DRVSPACE.000. This last file is a compressed one that holds all of your other files, with space for more. Never try to delete or alter DRVSPACE in any way.

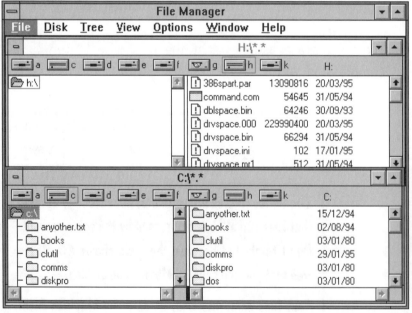

Take note

The total and free space size reports are identical but they look different because DOS shows the number of bytes and File Manager the number of Kb.

78

Notes

❑ Most of the files on drive H (or whatever letter is used) are hidden system files and you must not alter them in any way.

❑ The file called 386SPART.PAR is a Windows permanent swap file. This is set up using the **386** item in Windows **Control Panel** and opting for Virtual Memory. Windows-95 can set up this file on the compressed drive instead of in this uncompressed portion.

The most important point about using DriveSpace is that it seems to make no change at all, other than allowing more storage space, unless you need to do something advanced, such as changing the size of the Windows permanent swap file.

As far as you are concerned, then, all that has changed is that you have considerably more space on your hard drive, and it hasn't cost you a penny. If you have more than one hard drive, you can use the Custom option of DRVSPACE to set up this drive also, and the process is really no more difficult than using the Express option for the main hard drive.

Take note

Do not even try to read the file **DRVSPACE.OOO**, because it is in a coded format that you cannot read other than by the automatic action of DriveSpace.

Tip

You can use DriveSpace on floppies, converting the ordinary 1.4M floppy into something closer to 2.7M. The difference is useful, and because DriveSpace can be set to recognise the difference between a 1.4M and a DriveSpaced floppy, it needs no extra effort to use such floppies.

Floppy DriveSpace

It might look rather perverse to talk about DriveSpace on a floppy when this book is concerned with hard drives, but the two go together. DriveSpaced floppies make it easier to save a useful number of files on a floppy, and the reason you have so many files to save is because you are using a hard drive.

When you start DriveSpace you will see your hard drive listed as the only compressed drive.

1 Insert an ordinary formatted 1.4M floppy in the drive.

2 Quit Windows and start DRVSPACE from the DOS directory.

3 Open the **Compress** menu, and select **Existing drive** (as drive A: already exists).

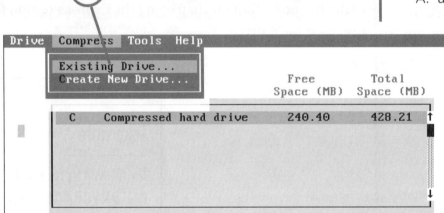

(3) Select Compress – Existing Drive

```
 Drive  Compress  Tools  Help
         Existing Drive...
         Create New Drive...              Free        Total
                                      Space (MB)   Space (MB)

    C      Compressed hard drive      240.40       428.21  ↑




                                                            ↓

 To work with a compressed drive, press the UP ARROW or DOWN
 ARROW key to select it. Then, choose the action you want
 from the Drive or Tools menu.

 To quit DriveSpace, choose Exit from the Drive menu. For
 help, press F1.

 Converts a drive to a DriveSpace compressed drive
```

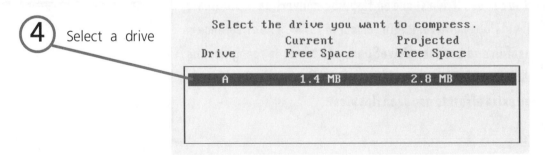

(4) Select a drive

```
         Select the drive you want to compress.
                      Current          Projected
         Drive      Free Space        Free Space

           A         1.4 MB            2.8 MB
```

80

It is rare for a floppy not to pass the surface scan test.

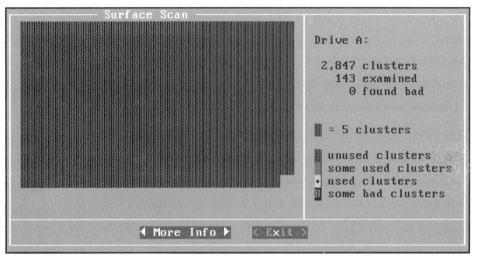

```
                    Surface Scan
                                          Drive A:

                                           2,847 clusters
                                             143 examined
                                               0 found bad


                                          ▓ = 5 clusters

                                          ▓ unused clusters
                                          ░ some used clusters
                                          · used clusters
                                          B some bad clusters

              ◄ More Info ►   ‹ Exit ›
```

4 The program scans all drives, and gives a report for Drive A:, showing the estimated space gain. If you have more than just A: and C:, select the drive to compress

Drive	Description	Free Space (MB)	Total Space (MB)
A	Compressed floppy disk	2.64	2.64
C	Compressed hard drive	240.34	428.27

5 The floppy is given a full surface scan, to check that DriveSpace can safely be used.

After several minutes, you will see the floppy listed along with the hard drive as a compressed drive.

Take note

It is only this floppy which is compressed, and this does not automatically compress every floppy in the A drive.

Take note

In Windows 3.1, trying to read a write-protected Drive Spaced floppy that has directories will make the computer black out - nothing appears on the screen, no key has any effect. You have to switch off, losing any data that was not saved to disk.

Automount

The older method for working with DriveSpaced floppy disks was that such a disk had to be 'mounted' by using the DRVSPACE program and clicking on the Mount option in the Drive menu. The disk could then be used, and **Drive – Unmount** was used before removing the disk.

This is no longer necessary, though the commands are still available, because you can now set DriveSpace so that compressed floppies are automatically recognised and mounted. This is done with **Tools – Options**.

1 After you have Drive-Spaced the floppy, keep it in the drive.

2 Open the **Tools** item, and select **Options**.

3 In the **Options** panel, click on **Enable Automounting** so that a cross shows.

4 The other two items should already be crossed by default, but if you never used DoubleSpace you can remove the cross against **Read DoubleSpace drives**.

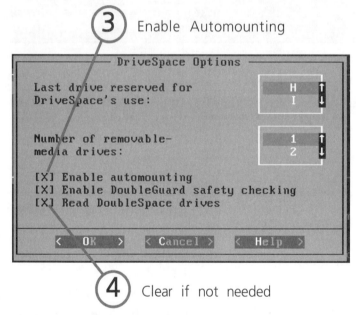

③ Enable Automounting

④ Clear if not needed

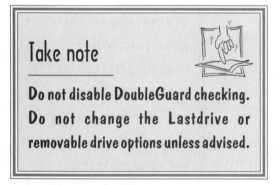

Take note

Do not disable DoubleGuard checking. Do not change the Lastdrive or removable drive options unless advised.

Tip

If you exchange disks with anyone who uses the older DoubleSpace system, keep this option crossed so that you can read such disks.

Basic steps

1 Start DriveSpace with a compressed floppy in the drive. Disable Automounting, and use **Unmount** to ensure that the floppy is not recognised as a compressed one.

2 Create a directory, called DRVSPACE on the hard drive.

3 Use DOS or the File Manager to copy DRVSPACE.000 from the floppy to the DBLFLOP directory.

4 Go back to DriveSpace and **Enable Automounting**.

5 Each time you want to DriveSpace a new formatted floppy, simply copy the DRVSPACE.000 file to the floppy.

Floppy hints

When you use automatic mounting and a set of DriveSpaced floppies, the effect is as if you had installed a 2.8M floppy drive. The only snag is that each floppy disk must be 'formatted' with DriveSpace, and the procedure is a lengthy one, as you will know by now. The steps on the right show an undocumented alternative.

In theory, this corner cutting would cause problems if a poor-quality floppy was used. In practice, I have never encountered a bad floppy in the last four hundred I have used. As usual, however, it's your own responsibility, and you might like to use ScanDisk (see later) on some floppies to check that they are good.

② Create a temporary directory

⑤ Copy the DrvSpace file

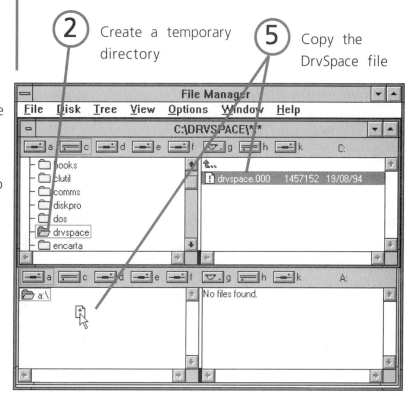

DriveSpace utilities

The main DriveSpace utilities in the **Tools** menu, apart from the Options, are concerned with defragmenting, uncompressing and checking disk condition.

- **Defragment** is used to defragment a drive that has been DriveSpaced. The normal DEFRAG program has little effect on a compressed drive.

- **Uncompress** is only an option if the disk is less than half full. You can save files to floppies (using a simple copy rather than Backup) and delete them from the hard drive if the disk is almost half-full.

- **Chkdsk** does not actually exist on modern versions of MS-DOS used with Windows, and if you select it you are asked to leave DRVSPACE and run SCANDISK. Later versions of DRVSPACE will allow you to run SCANDISK directly, and will be dealt with later.

- **Convert DoubleSpace** is useful only if you have a floppy or hard drive that used DoubleSpace

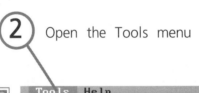

② Open the Tools menu

Take note

Do not DriveSpace disks for use with MWBACKUP or MSBACKUP. They both compress the files and must use uncompressed disks.

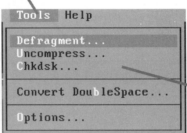

③ Click to select

Basic steps

1 Make sure you have shut down Windows or DOSSHELL, and you are in the DOS directory.

2 Run DRVSPACE, and click on the **Tools** menu.

3 Click on the option that you want to use.

Tip

Either avoid using the write-protect tab on DriveSpaced floppies, or label such floppies with a reminder that the tab must be closed before using the disk.

84

Basic steps

1 Quit Windows or DOSSHELL and use DrvSpace to show how the C: drive is used.

2 Look at the amount of uncompressed space. If your hard drive was larger than 250 Mbyte, there will be a substantial amount of uncompressed space.

4 Use **Compress – Create New Drive** and indicate how much of this space to convert to a compressed drive.

Create a new drive

DriveSpace has a limit of 500 Mbyte, so that if your one and only hard drive is of 500 Mbyte you will not get 1000 Mbyte on using DriveSpace. What you will get is about 500 Mbyte of compressed drive, and about 250 Mbyte of uncompressed drive left over.

You can use **Compress New Drive** on this left-over space, creating a new compressed drive with another drive letter. This has the minor disadvantage of your having to use more than one drive letter, though this can be turned to advantage by using one drive letter for programs and the other for data.

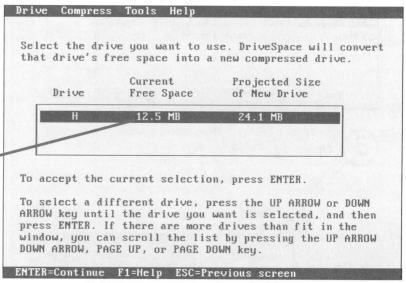

② Check the amount of free space

④ Create a New Drive

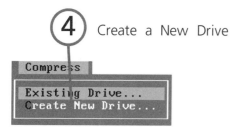

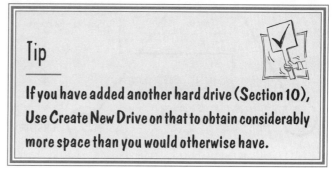

Tip

If you have added another hard drive (Section 10), Use Create New Drive on that to obtain considerably more space than you would otherwise have.

DriveSpace in Windows 95

DriveSpace is much better catered for in Windows 95, and you do not have to leave Windows to carry out DriveSpace actions.

All of your DriveSpace actions, as described for Windows 3.1, are now carried out using the DriveSpace option in System Tools.

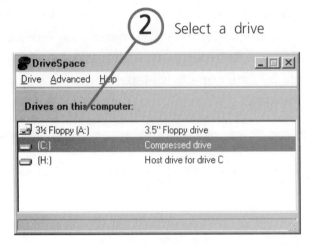

② Select a drive

③ Open the Drive menu

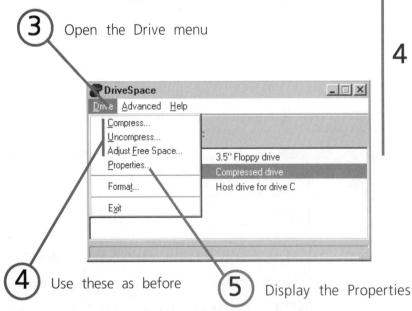

④ Use these as before   ⑤ Display the Properties

1 Move the pointer to the **System Tools** set as before, and click on **DriveSpace**. You will see an analysis of the drives you have on your computer.

2 Select a drive to work on. **C:** is the default, and the illustration shows this reported as a compressed drive.

❑ The floppy drive will also appear if there is a disk in the drive.

3 Open the **Drive** menu to find the main DriveSpace actions.

4 Use the **Compress**, **Uncompress** and **Adjust Free Space** options as for the older version.

Basic steps

5 Click **Properties** to display the way that the drive is used.

6 Check the option to **Hide host drive**, to ensure that this drive letter does not appear in Explorer or File Manager. This helps to avoid interfering with the DriveSpace file arrangement.

7 The other options are contained in the **Advanced** menu, and their actions correspond with those of the older version.

The main improvements for DriveSpace in Windows '95 are that the menus lead to illustrated panels that make the actions much easier to understand.

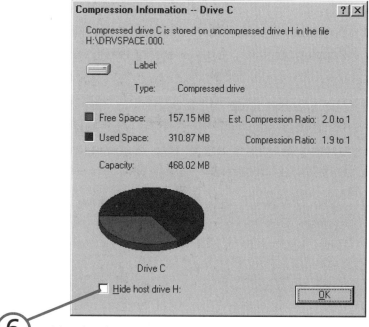

⑥ Hide the host

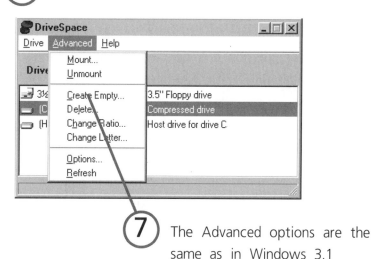

⑦ The Advanced options are the same as in Windows 3.1

Summary

❑ You always need more memory and disk space. As it happens, you can **increase the effective size of your hard drive** by using file compression in the form of the DriveSpace utility of MS-DOS.

❑ DriveSpace can be used on the **hard drive** and on **floppies**, and its benefits are obtained whether you use DOS or Windows.

❑ The **Express Setup** of DriveSpace is fast and useful for configuring your hard drive. You must not be running Windows at the time of using the DRVSPACE program.

❑ Using DRVSPACE will cause **a new drive letter** to appear. This represents the uncompressed hard drive, so that C: is still used for your hard drive files.

❑ A few **vital files** are held in uncompressed form

❑ You can find the theoretical and actual **compression ratios** for your files. If you alter the theoretical figure so that it equals the practical figure your available size information will be more accurate.

❑ **Floppy compression** can be carried out by simply copying the DRVSPACE.000 file to the floppy.

❑ DRVSPACE contains **utilities** for defragmenting, uncompressing and checking the condition of drives.

❑ You can also use the **Create New Drive** option to make use of space on a hard drive that has not been used before, or for an additional hard drive.

❑ **Windows 95** contains an improved version of the DriveSpace program which can be used within Windows.

7 Disk repairs

Disk problems

No hard drive is ever totally free from problems. Even when a drive is new there may be a few 'dead' spots where nothing can be saved. These are detected when the hard drive is formatted, and once detected they will be avoided, so that they do not cause problems.

Other problems can arise during use. The most common of these is 'lost clusters'. These arise from a file that has become fragmented when the information that leads from one part to another becomes erased. Such files are often unwanted, but because they do not appear on any directory display you cannot delete them or do anything with them. A cluster is a group of bytes.

If you install an additional hard drive that has not been formatted you will need to format it. Assuming that this drive is the D: drive, use the normal Windows 3.1 or Windows 95 Format procedure. See the Made Simple book for your version of Windows for details. The process takes some time for a large capacity drive.

Always check before formatting to see if the drive is formatted. If you can display a directory (even though it will probably be empty) then the drive is formatted and you do not need to format it again.

Points

❑ A hard drive is normally formatted only once in its life – when you put it into service. Some drives come ready-formatted so that you do not need to format them.

❑ Lost clusters often occur after you have had an extensive session of deleting old files. They can be a nuisance in two ways. One is that they take up disk space, the other is that they can become linked with other files.

❑ Magnetic media are of such good quality now that it is very rare to encounter other problems. When you do, the main diagnostic and repair utilities are CHKDSK and SCANDISK.

Basic steps

Using CHKDSK

1 Give the command
CHKDSK

to search the current
drive for faults.

2 After CHKDSK has run
you will see a report,
and get report on bad
portions or lost bits of
files, referred to as
allocation units.

3 The message that is
illustrated here shows
some lost allocation
units. If you are using
CHKDSK from DOS
these are probably
genuinely lost and you
need to mop them up.

CHKDSK is the older form of disk checker, and if you have
the later DOS versions 6.1 onwards you should use the
SCANDISK utility in preference to CHKDSK, because
SCANDISK is much more comprehensive and thorough.

You can use CHKDSK purely as a diagnostic either from
DOS or from Windows.

```
    5 lost allocation units found in 3 chains.
       40,960 bytes disk space would be freed

449,413,120 bytes total disk space
  1,572,864 bytes in 7 hidden files
  1,146,880 bytes in 139 directories
194,928,640 bytes in 3,584 user files
251,723,776 bytes available on disk

      8,192 bytes in each allocation unit
     57,693 total allocation units on disk
     33,561 available allocation units on disk

    655,360 total bytes memory
    557,984 bytes free
```

Take note

You need to heed a message like this if you have been using
CHKDSK from DOS. If you have been using CHKDSK from
Windows, take it with a pinch of salt, and try again after leaving
Windows. The way that Windows leaves files open so that it
can juggle with several at once looks like a fault to CHKDSK.

NEVER use the CHKDSK /F version of the command from
inside Windows.

Fixing with Chkdsk

The version of CHKDSK that will fix faults as well as diagnosing them is CHKDSK /F. You must never use this form from Windows or DOSSHELL, only from DOS.

Even on a large hard drive, CHKDSK does not take long, and it can be used on a hard drive that has been DriveSpaced. It is very much better, however, to use SCANDISK for such drives, and if DriveSpace is present in your DOS directory SCANDISK will also be there.

● If you use CHKDSK on a modern DOS you will be reminded that SCANDISK is much more comprehensive and useful.

```
1 lost allocation units found in 1 chains.
    8,192 bytes disk space would be freed

449,396,736 bytes total disk space
  1,581,056 bytes in 8 hidden files
  1,146,880 bytes in 139 directories
194,936,832 bytes in 3,584 user files
251,723,776 bytes available on disk

      8,192 bytes in each allocation unit
     52,693 total allocation units on disk
     13,563 available allocation units on disk

    655,360 total bytes memory
    557,984 bytes free
```

③ Is any space locked up in lost units?

1 Quit Windows.

2 Make the DOS directory current, type:

   CHKDSK /F

   and press **[Enter]**.

3 Wait until the message appears about any lost portions of files. You may be asked if you want to save these bits in a new file. This is useful only if the bits are of text files and if you need them.

❑ If you do not opt to save the pieces in a file they will be deleted.

Take note

You can also use **CHKDSK** on a set of files to find if they are fragmented.

Basic steps

Working with SCANDISK

1 Quit Windows.

2 Make the DOS directory current, type:

    SCANDISK

and press **[Enter]**.

3 If the disk is DriveSpaced, you will be asked if you want to check the 'host' first. This is the physical hard drive used for the compressed files. Always go for this option.

4 If you do not use DriveSpace SCANDISK will start on the C: drive right away.

❑ You do not need to specify any options with SCANDISK. These will be presented after the first scan is complete.

SCANDISK is a greatly improved utility for disk diagnosis and repair, and it should be used in preference to CHKDSK. Another advantage of using SCANDISK is that it will also deal sensibly with compressed disks using DriveSpace.

The illustrations here deal with the use of SCANDISK on a compressed hard drive. The screens and messages are much the same as you will see for an uncompressed drive, except that SCANDISK treats the compressed drive as if it were two drives, in this case C: and H:

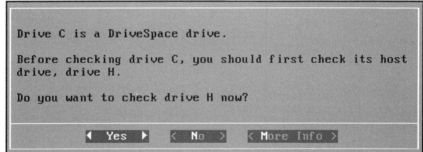

Drive C is a DriveSpace drive.

Before checking drive C, you should first check its host drive, drive H.

Do you want to check drive H now?

◄ Yes ►   ‹ No ›   ‹ More Info ›

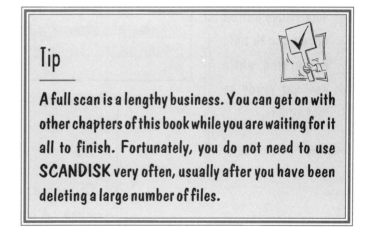

Tip

A full scan is a lengthy business. You can get on with other chapters of this book while you are waiting for it all to finish. Fortunately, you do not need to use **SCANDISK** very often, usually after you have been deleting a large number of files.

Scanning

When scanning starts, on the host drive H in the example, you will see a progress report appearing so that you can monitor the various aspects of your drive.

The File Allocation Tables are a set of numbers that tell the disk controller where a file is stored. Any problems with these will cause files to be lost, but SCANDISK can fix these faults, using a second copy of the F.A.T.

Some aspects of the scan can be very rapid, and the longest wait is for a surface scan.

Likely faults

- ❑ If there are any faults, they are usually in the file allocation tables (FAT), directory structure, or File system of the disk.

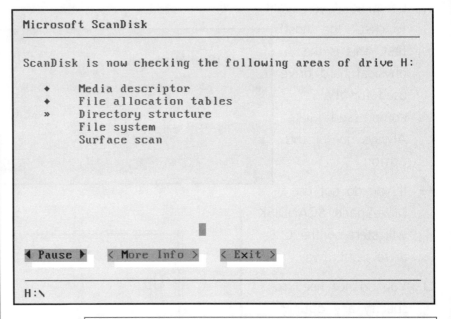

```
Microsoft ScanDisk


ScanDisk is now checking the following areas of drive H:

        ◆       Media descriptor
        ◆       File allocation tables
        »       Directory structure
                File system
                Surface scan




                                    ▮

    ◀ Pause ▶      < More Info >      < Exit >

H:\
```

Tip

The Pause button allows you to hold everything while you get ready to make notes.

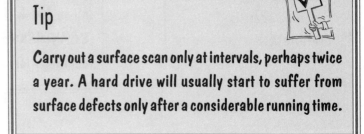

Tip

Carry out a surface scan only at intervals, perhaps twice a year. A hard drive will usually start to suffer from surface defects only after a considerable running time.

DriveSpace Scans

When SCANDISK starts on the DriveSpaced file there are more items to be checked.

These are all important, but it is unusual to find faults in some of the items. The important point is that SCANDISK checks much more than CHKDSK ever did, and can fix faults that CHKDSK could not touch.

The filenames will appear during the check on the directory structure, as illustrated above, so that you can see how the scan is progressing.

As for the earlier run on drive H, you do not need to run a surface scan each time you use SCANDISK.

The file header check ensures that the compressed file is recognised.

The directory structure, file system and file allocation table checks ensures that the individual files can be used.

```
Microsoft ScanDisk
_____

ScanDisk is now checking the following areas of drive C:

    ♦       DriveSpace file header
    »       Directory structure
            File system
            DriveSpace file allocation table
            Compression structure
            Volume signatures
            Boot sector
            Surface scan




    ◄ Pause ►    < More Info >    < Exit >
    _____       _____

_____
C:\MSOFFICE\POWERPNT\TEMPLATE\BWOVRHD
```

The next three checks make certain that minor damage can be repaired.

Fixing a fault

When SCANDISK finds a problem with a file it will give you the opportunity to fix it. You will see a notice that names the file and tells you that you can click on the Fix It button. It also tells you what will be done – in this example the damaged part of the file will be removed and the file altered so that it can be used. Simply removing damage will not, except for a text file, result in a file that is useable.

1 Look at the filename to determine the type of file.

❑ **Text** files can be patched up into something that you can read and use.

❑ Damaged **program** files (.COM or .EXE) are irrepairable.

❑ Repairing a PCX or other **graphics** file might leave a file that can be used after some editing.

2 Click **Fix It** if you think it is worth a try.

Take note

Usually when SCANDISK finds a damaged file, it's a file that you had deleted, and you don't need to recover it. You may get reports of cross-linked files that involve files that you do want to keep, but remember that repaired files are not always useful – it all depends on the type of files.

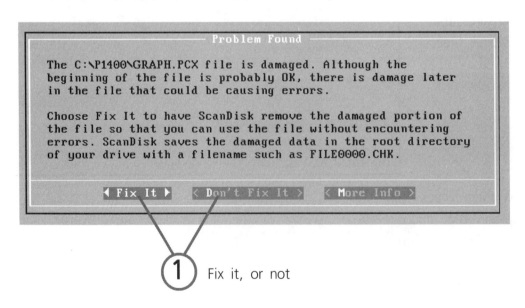

```
┌──────────────────── Problem Found ────────────────────┐
│                                                        │
│  The C:\P1400\GRAPH.PCX file is damaged. Although the  │
│  beginning of the file is probably OK, there is damage later │
│  in the file that could be causing errors.            │
│                                                        │
│  Choose Fix It to have ScanDisk remove the damaged portion of │
│  the file so that you can use the file without encountering │
│  errors. ScanDisk saves the damaged data in the root directory │
│  of your drive with a filename such as FILE0000.CHK.  │
│                                                        │
│      ◄ Fix It ►    ‹ Don't Fix It ›    ‹ More Info ›   │
└────────────────────────────────────────────────────────┘
```

 Fix it, or not

Clearing out scrap

Notes

1 These bits of files can be substantial – in this example about 1Mb.

2 You have to decide for yourself whether this might be useful.

3 If you have just repaired some files and find that you cannot get access to them take the **Save** option here.

4 Don't forget to look at the rest of the report if there is more to come.

Sometimes the use of SCANDISK will find fragments of files that cannot be identified. These usually result from some deletion actions in the past, and because they take up disk space you would prefer them to be removed.

There is a faint possibility, however, that the fragments are of something you did not mean to delete, and so SCANDISK gives you the chance to gather all the bits up into a file, give it a name, and make it accessible. This is useful only when the bits are mainly of text, because you can edit a text file and fit the bits together properly. Other files are not usually worth trying to recover.

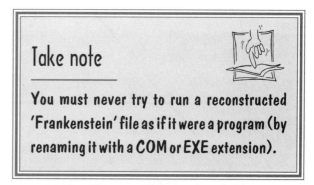

Take note

You must never try to run a reconstructed 'Frankenstein' file as if it were a program (by renaming it with a COM or EXE extension).

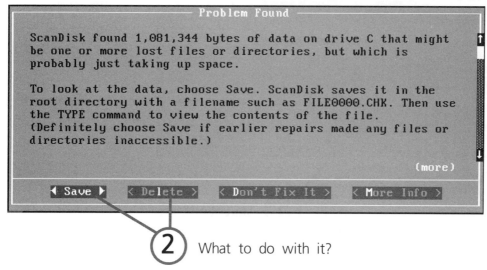

```
┌──────────────── Problem Found ────────────────┐
ScanDisk found 1,081,344 bytes of data on drive C that might
be one or more lost files or directories, but which is
probably just taking up space.

To look at the data, choose Save. ScanDisk saves it in the
root directory with a filename such as FILE0000.CHK. Then use
the TYPE command to view the contents of the file.
(Definitely choose Save if earlier repairs made any files or
directories inaccessible.)

                                                    (more)

 ◄ Save ►    < Delete >    < Don't Fix It >    < More Info >
```

2 What to do with it?

97

Windows 95 ScanDisk

As you would expect by now, you do not have to leave Windows 95 in order to use SCANDISK, and the new version is contained in the System Tools set.

If your hard drive uses DriveSpace you can opt to check the host drive (H: in this example) as well as the compressed file C:.

It is seldom worth while to check floppy disks unless you have a floppy that you cannot read because of some problems.

1 Move the pointer to **System Tools** and click on **ScanDisk**.

2 Select the drive – the hard drive is already selected as a default.

3 Choose your type of scan, **Standard** or **Thorough**. The Thorough test can take a considerable time.

4 Make sure that there is a tick against **Automatically Fix Errors**.

5 Click on the **Start** button to carry out the scan.

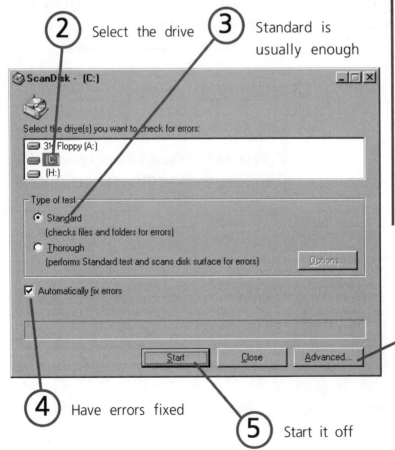

② Select the drive

③ Standard is usually enough

④ Have errors fixed

⑤ Start it off

The Advanced options are worth looking at

Basic steps

1 In the **Display summary** options, choose **Always** to ensure that you get news, whether good or bad.

2 Leave **Lost file fragments** at he default of **Convert to files**. That way you can see if they contain anything useful.

3 Set the **Log file** (the record of the result) to **Replace.** Only use **Append** if you suspect that the disk is deteriorating.

4 In the **Check files for** options, **Invalid name** checking is all you normally need.

5 In **Cross-linked files** choose **Make copies**. This offers some chance of recovering information from files that have become connected.

Advanced options

The panel of ScanDisk contains a button labelled Advanced. This provides a new panel with some useful options.

Note that when lost fragments of cross-linked files are recovered as new files, they are useful only if they were text files – you can try to read them with NotePad or WordPad. If they were not text files, delete them.

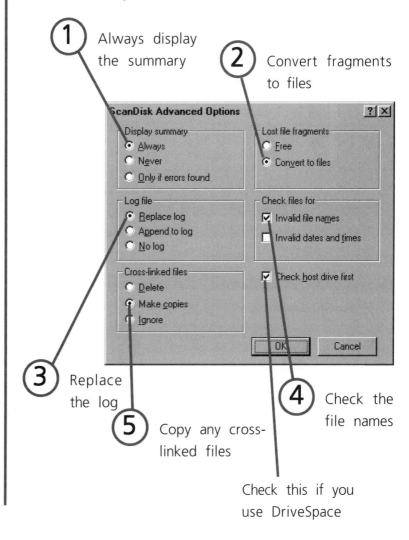

① Always display the summary

② Convert fragments to files

③ Replace the log

④ Check the file names

⑤ Copy any cross-linked files

Check this if you use DriveSpace

Summary

❑ Hard drives are never totally free from faults, but when you put a drive into service, only the fault-free parts are used. During service, portions of files can accumulate – these are referred to as **lost clusters**.

❑ On older DOS versions the **CHKDSK** utility can be used, after quitting Windows 3.1, to find and gather these lost clusters. freeing up disk space.

❑ The command **CHKDSK /F** will fix faults as it finds them.

❑ **SCANDISK** is a more modern utility for checking the hard drive, and it will first report on the condition of the drive. Once again, you must not be running Windows 3.1.

❑ SCANDISK can carry out a large number of checks on a hard drive and also on a compressed file. It can also do a **full surface scan** of the disk, looking for faults that have developed since the disk was put into service.

❑ Windows 95 contains its own version of SCANDISK that can be used within Windows.

8 Undelete

Where did it go?

What happens when you delete a file or a directory? Its name vanishes from the directory display, and the available disk space rises so that you can save more files in that space. Take a look at the steps of deleting a file.

Because the bytes of the file are still on the disk, any file can be un-deleted. At one time this was a highly-skilled action that needed an expert, using the DEBUG program, some calculations, muttering into beard, and a bit of luck; hey presto – your file was recovered.

Nowadays it's a lot easier using the MWUNDEL program that you should have in a group somewhere. This program is in the DOS directory, not in C:\WINDOWS, and it is installed from MS-DOS 6.22.

Windows 95 doesn't need any of this. Unwanted files are sent to the Recycling Bin, and can be recovered if you haven't emptied the bin. See Section 3 for details.

MWUNDEL

1 The first letter of the name is replaced by an 'invisible' character, code 229 – this is the signal to MS-DOS that the file is not wanted again.

2 The space that the file has used is added to the list of available space.

3 That's it! The bytes of the file, apart from the first character in the name, are untouched.

4 The file is therefore still present on the hard drive, and will remain there until another file is saved in the same space.

5 Even if another file is saved, it might not totally wipe out all of the 'deleted' file.

Basic steps

1 Open the Main group of Windows 3.1. Run **Windows Setup**.

2 Select **Setup Applications**.

3 Select the option to **specify an application**.

4 Type in the name, or use **Browse**, to select the MWUNDEL.EXE program.

You will need to install Windows Undelete if you cannot find it in any of your groups. Check first that the program MWUNDEL.EXE is in your C:\DOS directory. If it is not you will need to put it in from your MS-DOS distribution disks – remember that this requires you to run Setup, unless you know how to use the EXPAND.EXE program on the compressed version of the file that is on the MS-DOS distribution floppy number 3.

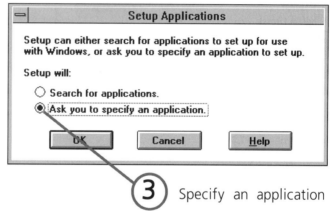

(3) Specify an application

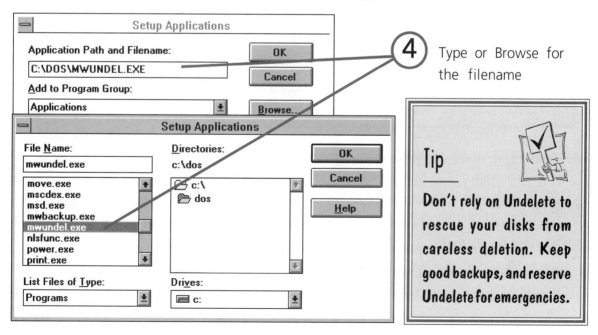

(4) Type or Browse for the filename

Tip

Don't rely on Undelete to rescue your disks from careless deletion. Keep good backups, and reserve Undelete for emergencies.

Group and icon

The last stage of setting up the Undelete application is to create an icon for it in a Program Manager Group. You can also change the icon if you like.

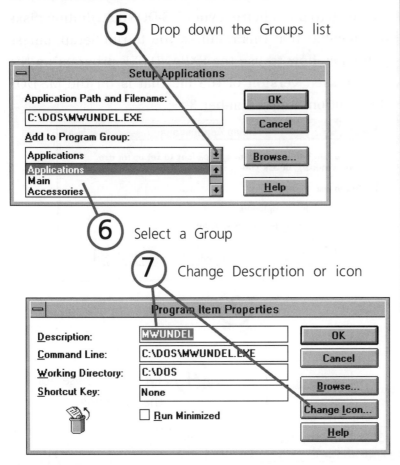

⑤ Drop down the Groups list

Setup Applications

Application Path and Filename:

C:\DOS\MWUNDEL.EXE

Add to Program Group:

Applications

Applications
Main
Accessories

OK
Cancel
Browse...
Help

⑥ Select a Group

⑦ Change Description or icon

Program Item Properties

Description: MWUNDEL
Command Line: C:\DOS\MWUNDEL.EXE
Working Directory: C:\DOS
Shortcut Key: None

☐ Run Minimized

OK
Cancel
Browse...
Change Icon...
Help

Tip

Practice using Undelete on some files that do not matter, so you know what to do when it's important. You can practice on a floppy rather than on the hard drive.

5 Drop down the list of Groups – if you want to use a new Group you need to create it first (see *Windows Made Simple*).

6 Select a Group. The program and its icon will be added to it. The default is Applications Group.

7 You can change the icon or the description by selecting item in Program Manager and using **File – Properties**

Take note

If you intend to work from **DOS**, you cannot use **MWUNDEL**, but you will find **UNDELETE.EXE** in the **C:\DOS** directory. (See page 114)

Using MWUNDEL

1 Double-click on the MWUNDEL icon.

2 You will see the MWUNDEL panel appear. By default this will show the C:\ directory, and any deleted files will appear.

Before you start, remember that Undelete has a good chance of succeeding only if nothing has been saved since the deletion action. There is a moderate chance otherwise, and absolutely none at all if the disk has been defragmented since the deletion. Undelete will tell you what the chances are of recovering a named file.

In this example, the file condition is shown as Good. This is all right for a text file, but it would be distinctly dodgy if you were trying to recover, for example, a program file or an Excel workbook file.

Change to another **drive** or **directory** if needed

Sort the files into order of name, type, date, etc.

Find a particular file (see page 108)

Print the list of deleted files

Undelete is greyed out until a file is selected

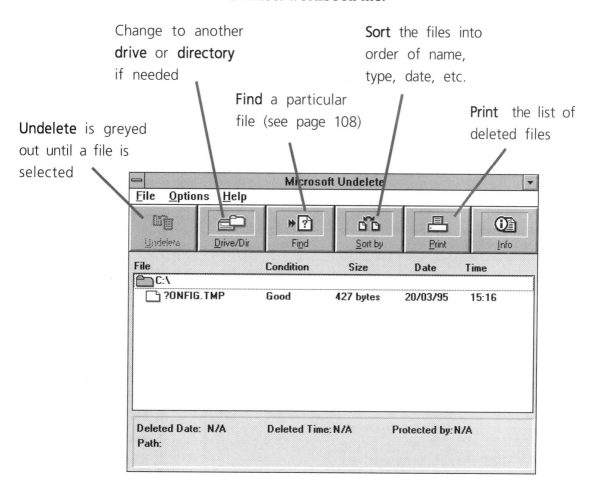

Undeleting

Let's leave the details out for the moment. Suppose you use the Drive/Dir option to get to a directory where you know you have been deleting files. What you need to do is to select a file or files and click on Undelete.

1 Use **Drive/Dir** to get to the directory where you know deleted files exist.

2 Select one you want to restore from the list of deleted files.

3 Click on the **Undelete** button.

4 Type in the first letter of the file name and click **OK**.

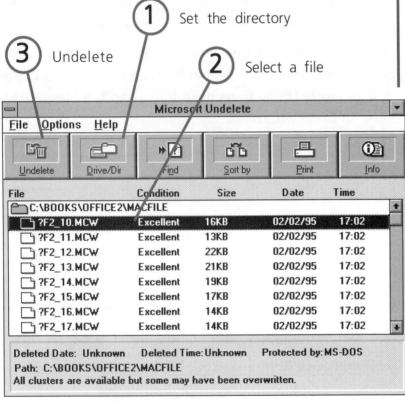

① Set the directory

③ Undelete

② Select a file

④ Give a first letter

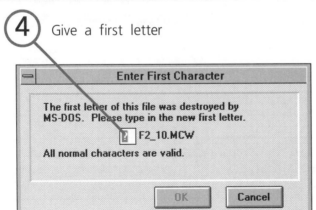

Take note

You do not need to type the same first letter – any character will do if you have forgotten the old version. The only essential thing is to type in something.

Basic steps

1 Select a file.

2 Click on the **Info** button for the more detailed report on the state of the file.

❑ In this example another file has been saved over the deleted file, and the contents will be corrupted.

What are the chances?

The MWUNDEL lists show the Condition of deleted files. This is a good guide to the chances of restoring them successfully.

Excellent – the files are intact, and all that needs to be done is to restore the first letter of the name, and make some calculations (all done by MWUNDEL). Even if the files were program files, you can probably recover them and use them.

Good – worth recovering if they were of text, but it would be risky to try to recover program files.

Poor – worth recovering only if they are text files and valuable. They will need editing to check that nothing is missing or corrupted.

Destroyed – and impossible to recover.

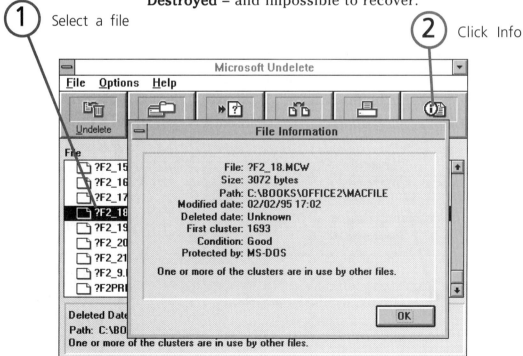

① Select a file

② Click Info

File Information

File: ?F2_18.MCW
Size: 3072 bytes
Path: C:\BOOKS\OFFICE2\MACFILE
Modified date: 02/02/95 17:02
Deleted date: Unknown
First cluster: 1693
Condition: Good
Protected by: MS-DOS

One or more of the clusters are in use by other files.

Finding deleted files

What if you cannot find the files? One chance is that you can find them using the Find button of MWUNDEL. This allows you to specify files either by using a filename or part of a filename (you can use the usual wildcard characters of * or ? in the name that you type), or by typing some text that was contained in the file and which would identify it.

A search that covers all of the hard drive can take some time, but the action is fast enough to ensure that you can wait for it – it's nothing like as slow as waiting for a surface scan from SCANDISK, for example.

1 Click the Find icon

2 Type the **File specification**, using wildcards to stand for unknown parts of the name.

3 If you know a key word in a text file, type it in the Containing slot.

4 Set the **Ignore Case** or **Whole Word** options, if possible, to narrow down your search.

5 Click **OK**

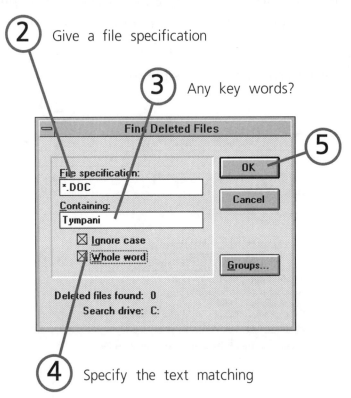

② Give a file specification

③ Any key words?

⑤ Start it off

④ Specify the text matching

Take note

If you have deleted a directory along with files, undelete the directory first. MWUNDEL will show a deleted directory in its list.

Basic steps

Sort and Select

□ **Search Groups**

1 Click the **Groups** button in the Find dialog box to restrict the search to selected groups of files.

2 Click the **Edit** button to specify groups or parts of groups for yourself.

□ **Sorted displays**

1 Click the **Sort By** icon in the main window.

2 Select the criteria by which to sort the list.

□ Note that this allows you to list files by **Condition** as well as by the usual criteria.

You can restrict the scope of the search to selected Groups. In addition, you can set the Sort by option. This allows you to specify how the deleted files are displayed, and it is particularly useful if you are using a wildcard search which might turn up a large number of files.

② Add or remove groups from the Search list

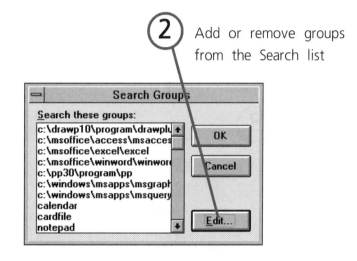

② Select a Sort order

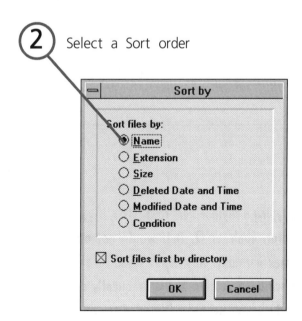

Take Note

The option of sorting by directory first is a useful one – you should retain it.

Protection levels

MWUNDEL offers several levels of protection that you can set.

The **Standard** level of protection is, as this Section has demonstrated, useful and not difficult to work with — it only requires you to supply a first character for each filename, and that character need not be the original.

Tracker and **Sentry** are the other two levels of Undeletion. Both require disk and memory space, but Tracker requires only a very small amount of disk space.

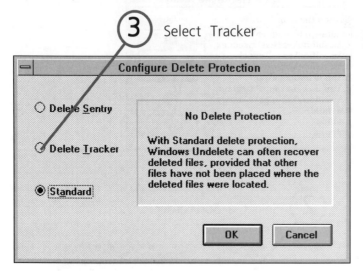

(3) Select Tracker

Configure Delete Protection

○ Dele**te Sentry**

◐ Delete **T**racker

● Standard

No Delete Protection

With Standard delete protection, Windows Undelete can often recover deleted files, provided that other files have not been placed where the deleted files were located.

[OK]   [Cancel]

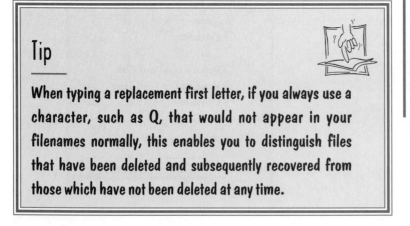

Tip

When typing a replacement first letter, if you always use a character, such as Q, that would not appear in your filenames normally, this enables you to distinguish files that have been deleted and subsequently recovered from those which have not been deleted at any time.

Basic steps

1 Open the Options menu in MWUNDEL.

2 Select **Configure Delete Protection**.

❏ The default protection level is **Standard**. This is perfectly acceptable unless you are likely delete valuable files that you have not backed up and whose names you have forgotten.

3 Click on **Delete Tracker**, then on **OK**.

4 Select which drive(s) you want to protect.

5 Click on **OK**.

❏ You will be reminded that Tracker cannot be activated until the computer is rebooted. The AUTOEXEC.BAT file will be changed, adding the line UNDELETE /LOAD

Tracker

Tip

You do not need the protection level of Sentry or Tracker if you use a good backup system. Extra protection is only necessary if the computer is used by several people who create and delete a large number of files each day.

Tracker works by keeping a small file of deleted files with their locations on the disk. This allows for quick and easy undeleting, but the files can still be corrupted by saving other files after deleting the old ones. Only the Sentry level of MWUNDEL can cope with this problems and allow complete recovery. Even SENTRY has its limits, however.

④ Click to select drives

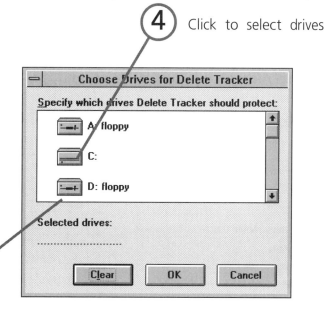

Only hard and floppy drives are shown, as files cannot be deleted from a CD-ROM

Take note

The MS-DOS UNDELETE can sometimes recover text data from files that MWUNDEL classes as Poor or Destroyed. It's useful as a last-chance method.

111

Using Sentry

The Sentry system operates by keeping a hidden directory that is used to hold deleted files. You can opt for what maximum number of files to hold or for how long files should be retained before being finally deleted (purged).

Sentry will hold files intact despite later file saving, but because your hard drive space is limited you must specify limits to what you retain in this way.

Only files protected by Sentry are classed as Perfect and can always be recovered in perfect condition.

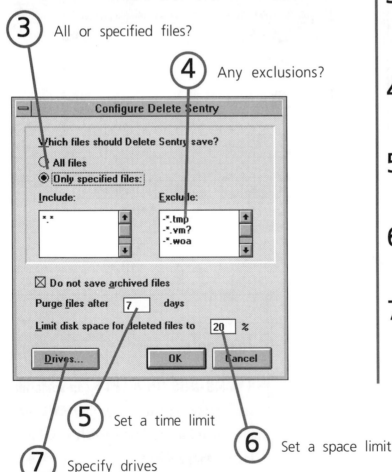

3 All or specified files?

4 Any exclusions?

5 Set a time limit

6 Set a space limit

7 Specify drives

1 Open the **Options** menu of MWUNDEL and select **Configure Delete Protection**.

2 Opt for **Sentry**.

You will see the SENTRY configuration dialog box.

3 Select either **All files** or **Only specified files** (such as *.DOC and *.PCX) to guard.

4 Select any extensions to **Exclude** types of files from SENTRY

5 Set the number of **days**, after which files will be **purged**.

6 Set a **Limit** to the **disk space** to be used in this way.

7 Click the **Drives** button and specify which drives to use with SENTRY.

112

❑   As before, you are advised that the protection will not start until the computer has been re-booted. The AUTOEXEC.BAT file is changed with a new UNDELETE line.

The way that Tracker or Sentry is used is defined in a file called UNDELETE.INI which is held in the C:\DOS directory. The line UNDELETE /LOAD in AUTOEXEC.BAT ensures that the Undelete method to be used is set at start up. If the file is not loaded because the UNDELETE /LOAD line is missing, the Standard MS-DOS method will be used rather than Sentry or Tracker.

```
==                    Notepad - UNDELETE.INI
File   Edit   Search   Help
d.sentry=FALSE
d.tracker=FALSE

[mirror.drives]
C=

[sentry.drives]
C=

[sentry.files]
sentry.files=*.DOC *.PCX -*.tmp -*.vm? -*.woa -*.swp -*.spl

[configuration]
archive=FALSE
days=7
```

Sentry maintenance

You can also purge the Sentry directory files manually, by selecting this option in the MWUNDEL menu. This avoids the disk becoming cluttered with unwanted files – if you are sure that they are unwanted.

Take note

When you use Sentry, you will find that the files that it creates are almost impossible to remove by normal methods. Do not use Sentry on floppy disks.

Using DOS UNDELETE

Basic steps

The DOS program UNDELETE.EXE is the method of undeletion if you are not using Windows, and it can sometimes recover files that the Windows version cannot cope with.

On the other hand, UNDELETE cannot restore directories, and if you have been deleting directories you need to use the Windows version, which allows you first to restore the directory name and then find the files for that directory.

UNDELETE uses the same type of UNDELETE.INI file as MWUNDEL to hold details of the settings for Sentry and Tracker.

1 Quit Windows (or DOSSHELL) and log to the C:\DOS directory.

2 Type

UNDELETE

followed by any options that you need (see opposite).

3 When a deleted file is found, type Y if you want to restore it and give a first letter for a filename.

```
UNDELETE - A delete protection facility
Copyright (C) 1987-1993 Central Point Software, Inc.
All rights reserved.

Directory: C:\TEMP
File Specifications: *.*

    Delete Sentry control file not found.

    Deletion-tracking file not found.

    MS-DOS directory contains   14 deleted files.
    Of those,   13 files may be recovered.

Using the MS-DOS directory method.

    ?WRF0004 TMP     1536 25/03/95  9:32   ...A  Undelete (Y/N)?y
    Please type the first character for ?WRF0004.TMP: w

File successfully undeleted.

    ?WRF0005 TMP        0 25/03/95  9:36   ...A  Undelete (Y/N)?←

C:\TEMP>
```

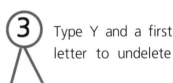

(3) Type Y and a first letter to undelete

If it has 0 bytes, there is nothing left to recover

Options

/LIST will list all the deleted files in the stated drive and directory but will not recover any.

/ALL will recover all the files in the specified directory without prompting. Sentry will be used if available, otherwise Tracker, otherwise the # sign (or another character) will be used for the first letter of each file.

Take note

Remember that nothing, absolutely nothing, can take the place of a good backup system. Actions such as Undelete and Unformat are for use in emergencies only.

The UNDELETE options

UNDELETE is normally followed by a path and filename, for example, using UNDELETE C:\BOOKS\CHAP1.DOC to undelete a specified file. You can also use a large number of option letters and words following a slash mark.

● Note that if you have deleted a directory, you cannot restore it with UNDELETE and you also cannot restore any files that were contained in that directory. If you cannot use MWUNDEL, it is sometimes possible to recover a directory that is a child of the root directory by using UNFORMAT, and then use UNDELETE to recover the files from that directory. Don't rely on it.

● On the other hand, some files that are marked as Poor by MWUNDEL can be restored in reasonable condition by UNDELETE.

Tracker and Sentry

The UNDELETE command can be followed by /S or /T to make use of Sentry or Tracker, as described earlier. For example, you can include the line:

    UNDELETE /S

in your AUTOEXEC.BAT, to install Sentry protection each time you boot the computer.

Summary

- ❏ **Delete** does not erase the bytes of a file from the disk, it only alters some codes in the directory. This allows for un-deleting files.

- ❏ **Undeletion** of a file is easiest if nothing else has been saved since the file was deleted.

- ❏ Windows 95 uses the **Recycling Bin** to hold unwanted files, and any file can be recovered after a Delete action, if the bin has not been emptied.

- ❏ **MWUNDEL** is used from Windows and **UNDELETE** is used from DOS.

- ❏ You need to **specify a directory** before you start MWUNDEL.

- ❏ At the simplest, if a file can be undeleted you are asked to supply a **first character** for the filename. MWUNDEL tells you the state of a 'deleted' file so that you can see if recovery is possible.

- ❏ MWUNDEL has a **Find** option so that you can look for deleted files.

- ❏ Two higher **levels of delete-protection** can be used. These are called Tracker and Sentry.

- ❏ **Tracker** requires little in the way of resources, and it avoids the need to supply a first character of the filename.

- ❏ **Sentry** offers a very high level of protection, but for a limited number of files.

- ❏ The DOS **UNDELETE** program is limited as far as undeleting directories, but it can be useful if you want to undelete all the files in a directory.

9 Viruses

Viruses

Don't panic!

Hard drive viruses are a menace which affect very few hard-disk users, but which, like terrorism, cause more worries and expense than damage. A virus is, strictly speaking, a piece of code which can attach itself to a program and reproduce itself so that it can be transmitted to other programs and also from one computer to another. The term is also used of other unwanted codes which can be loaded into a computer and which from then on will cause problems to appear, whether these can be spread to further computers or not.

Viruses reach your hard-drive program files either from a floppy disk that you have used to install something, or from a program that you have received by way of the modem and run. Files that contain only data will not pass a virus, and programs that you run from a floppy and which do not install anything on the hard drive are also innocent.

The main types of virus are the Boot Sector type which locates itself in the boot sector of the hard disk and loads in whenever the computer is booted, and the Parasitic virus, which is attached to a program file and is activated when that file is used.

The problem is not one that affects machines that run only floppy disks, because a floppy disk with a virus can be thrown away. Viruses are not effective on data files, because data files are not composed of instructions, so that the virus instruction cannot be executed. No virus has ever been found in the CMOS RAM memory of any PC computer.

❏ A virus can affect your computer only if you load and run a program from a disk that contains the virus, or load software over the telephone lines by way of a modem.

❏ Millions of computer users who do not use a modem and are careful about where they buy software are at no risk of virus infection.

❏ Many viruses are comparatively harmless, like graffiti and have been devised by programmers wishing to demonstrate their skills.

Don't get it!

- ❏ Beware of gifts of disks. Obtain programs only from reputable suppliers, whether commercial or shareware. Never run games that are passed on from another user.

- ❏ Try out suspect disks on a floppy-only machine if you can.

- ❏ Beware of demo disks or system checking disks that have been inserted into a large number of computers.

- ❏ Keep backups of all program files on floppy disks. If all else fails, you can reinstall a 'clean' program from these disks.

- ❏ If you download a program from the Internet, save it on a floppy and run it from the floppy, with the hard drive protected, until you are certain it is safe.

What do they do?

A virus may simply put up a message of the 'Kilroy was here' variety on your screen, but at the other end of the scale it may cause files to vanish from your hard disk directory. This damage is not necessarily irreversible, but even if it is not it can take a long time to sort out. The really destructive viruses are fortunately rare.

Bombs, also not necessarily viruses, come in two forms, time bombs and logic bombs. A bomb program, once loaded, saves itself on the disk and does nothing until some condition is met. A time-bomb will be activated by date (like Friday 13th) or time (like midnight) and will carry out its action if the computer is running at this time. A logic bomb will operate when other some conditions, such as 65% or more of the disk being used, or a copy of some well-known program being installed

The Trojan Horse is not really a virus, but it can cause just as serious problems. It takes the form of a program with an interesting title. When the program is loaded and run, it carries out the damage.

The Worm is also not really a virus but it reproduces itself within the computer that it affects until so many copies have been made that there is no further room on the hard disk. It also has a serious effect on networks.

Take note

The best way to deal with viruses is not to become infected.

The present problem

The earliest types of virus programs were comparatively simple. They usually altered the COMMAND.COM file, and could be counteracted by checking the size of this file regularly and re-installing if necessary.

Later types of viruses are much more ingenious, using a variety of techniques to conceal their presence and to evade virus-detecting software.

The sequence of bytes used by viruses can often be used to detect a virus, and some now use code that is varied each time the virus reproduces. A few portions, however, need to be kept in sequence and can be detected.

The MWAV program can be used from Windows 3.1 as a way of checking for and deterring the entry of a virus.

No Anti-virus program is nearly as effective as taking care not to become infected.

The filenames below should be found in your C:\DOS directory – they comprise the MWAV set for Windows 3.1. There is another MSAV set for DOS.

mwav.exe	142640	31/05/94	06:22:00	a
mwav.hlp	24619	31/05/94	06:22:00	a
mwavabsi.dll	54576	31/05/94	06:22:00	a
mwavdlg.dll	36368	31/05/94	06:22:00	a
mwavdosl.dll	44736	31/05/94	06:22:00	a
mwavdrvl.dll	7744	31/05/94	06:22:00	a
mwavmgr.dll	21712	31/05/94	06:22:00	a
mwavscan.dll	151568	31/05/94	06:22:00	a
mwavsos.dll	7888	31/05/94	06:22:00	a
mwavtsr.exe	17328	31/05/94	06:22:00	a

Points

❑ Some intercept the DIR command so as to show the original length of an infected program, and this interception can be used to affect any program that checks file length

❑ These methods cannot conceal the amount of memory that the infected program takes up in the computer, and this is one of the methods that is used by virus-detecting programs which will compare the length from a standard reading with the length of the file in the memory.

❑ A few rare viruses make use of features that are built into the processor and which can by-pass any detecting software.

1 Add the MWAV set into any Windows Group, following the same procedure as for MWUNDEL. You should end up with two new icons in the Group that you select.

2 You need also to maintain an up-to-date virus list. This can be updated by way of your modem. If you have no modem, that's one less reason to worry about viruses

When you set-up MS-DOS 6.22 (or any recent DOS) you will have been asked to opt for using either Windows or DOS anti-virus (also backup and undelete). If you opted for the Windows variety, it should have been installed automatically as part of the Applications group. If you opted for the MS-DOS variety you can run Anti-virus from DOS (after quitting Windows). You will still need the MSAVIRUS.LST file for either version.

There are two program files in the MWAV set:

 MWAV – the main virus checking file;

 MWAVTSR – used to try to detect actions that might be introducing a virus.

The basis for detecting a virus is a change in a program file, or some 'signature' of bits appearing in a program file. Since new viruses are being spread at intervals, you need to keep an updated file of data as part of your virus scanning software. This is the file MSAVIRUS.LST.

Detecting any attempt to install a virus is more difficult, because the actions that are used to install a program are also those that install a virus, but if you disable the detection when you are installing a legitimate program you should not be too troubled by false reports.

Starting MWAV

Note that you can start MWAV without any preparation, but you cannot use MWAVTSR unless you have installed VSAFE, see later.

(2) Select a drive

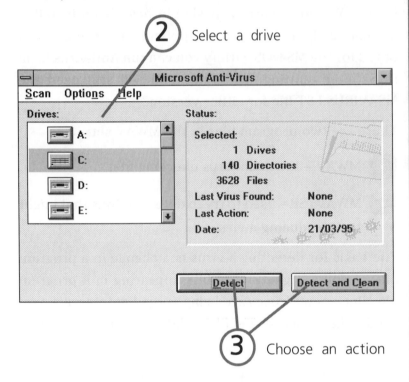

③ Choose an action

When you use Detect, you will see the memory scanned followed by a much longer scan for files. The files scan on a large hard drive allows you time for a coffee.

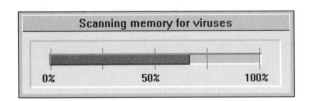

1 Double-click on the MWAV icon. This is usually placed in the Applications group. You will see the MWAV panel appear.

2 Select your drive by clicking on the drive icon – this will almost certainly be C:, but you might want to check a floppy in A: to find if it might contain a virus.

The program will read all the directories in the drive you have selected.

3 You can now opt to use **Detect** or **Detect and Clean**.

Take note

If this check reveals a virus, you can use **Detect and Clean** the next time round, and with luck this will eliminate the cause of the problem

Reporting

This is the result we all hope for – no infection. This does not prove that your drive has no viruses, only that none have been found. There is a difference. Unfortunately, not all anti-virus scans are equally efficient.

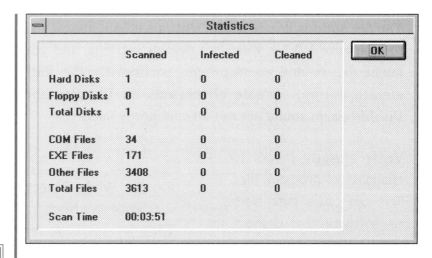

MSAV tries to identify viruses from its list of known types. You can click on Scan and then on Virus List to see (or print) the list of known viruses. The names (and spelling!) tell an interesting story about the type of people who create these programs.

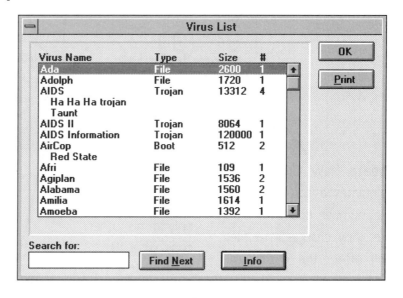

The Options

The Set options list, from the Options menu, allows you to configure MWAV. Keep the default settings, and you might like to add some others, particularly the **Anti-stealth** option. **Create checksums on floppies** and **Disable alarm sound** are not so commonly used.

Verify Integrity checks for changes on program files. This can cause false alarms on software that changes the main program when you alter its configuration. Modern software uses an INI file for settings and does not change the main program file.

Prompt While Detect will issue warnings when a virus is found, rather than wait until the end of the scan.

The **Stealth** type not only contains the virus itself but also methods of concealing the virus. For example, a DIR display will not show that the size of the file has changed, because the Stealth code takes over the DIR statistics.

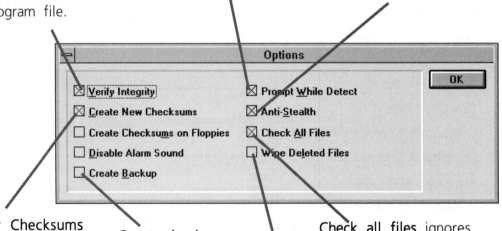

Create New Checksums calculates a total from all the number codes in a file. Any change in a file will affect the checksum.

Create backup should be used only if no other copy of a file exists – it is risky.

Check all files ignores extensions; if turned off, only COM, EXE and BAT files will be checked.

Wipe Deleted files should not be used unless you are experienced with MWAV.

1 Edit AUTOEXEC.BAT, adding the line

VSAFE

into the file (before the line that starts Windows).

2 Add the MWAVTSR icon to the Startup group of Windows

3 Next time you boot the computer, VSAFE will be running, and you can double-click MWAVTSR to configure it.

4 The defaults that are marked in for you are useful. You might want to add others for special reasons. For example, use **General Write Protect** on the hard drive when you run a suspect program on a floppy.

VSAFE will detect any form of SETUP program altering the hard drive. It is executed from the AUTOEXEC.BAT file, and remains in memory as a way of detecting viruses. It cannot be placed into AUTOEXEC.BAT from Windows, and the MWAVTSR program cannot be used from Windows until VSAFE is running.

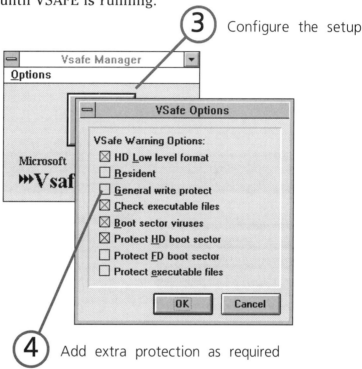

③ Configure the setup

④ Add extra protection as required

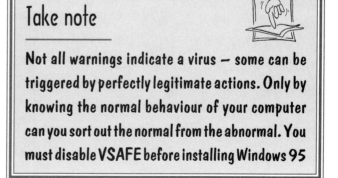

Take note

Not all warnings indicate a virus — some can be triggered by perfectly legitimate actions. Only by knowing the normal behaviour of your computer can you sort out the normal from the abnormal. You must disable VSAFE before installing Windows 95

MSAV

You can install the MSAV set of files from the MS-DOS distribution disks by using the SETUP program for MS-DOS, or by using the EXPAND command, which has already been illustrated.

The MSAV.EXE command is the main program file, which needs the MSAVIRUS.LST file for its list of viruses and their characteristics. The other two MSAV files are for the Help text.

The introductory screen of MSAV provides much the same set of options as MWAV.

1 Check that these MSAV files are in your DOS directory.

msav.exe	172198
msav.hlp	23891
msavhelp.ovl	29828
msavirus.lst	35520

2 If they are not, install them from the MS-DOS distribution disks.

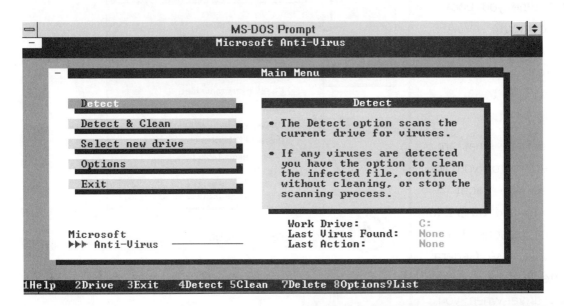

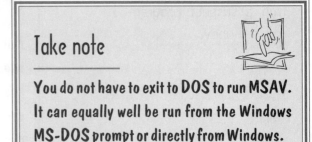

Take note

You do not have to exit to DOS to run MSAV. It can equally well be run from the Windows MS-DOS prompt or directly from Windows.

Basic steps

Using MSAV

1 **Select the drive** to use by moving the cursor to this option, pressing [Enter], and pointing to one of the drive letters which appear at the top left hand corner.

2 Use **Detect** only, or **Detect and Clean**. The action is faster than that of MWAV.

3 The **Options** menu provides the same options as for MWAV.

The use of MSAV runs very closely parallel to the use of MWAV, and the main difference is that the colour of screen lettering often makes it more difficult to see.

The various options are the same, but you can also use the F-keys to obtain the menu actions as follows:

[F1]	Help
[F2]	Drive selection (default is C:\)
[F3]	Exit back to DOS
[F4]	Detect only
[F5]	Detect and clean
[F7]	Delete checklist files
[F8]	Options (as for MWAV)
[F9]	List of viruses

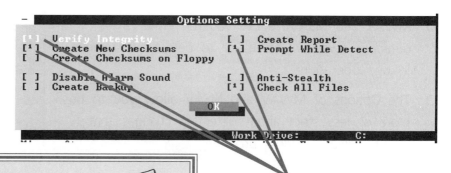

Select these options for safe and efficient operation

Tip

Because of the speed of MSAV you might want to run it before starting Windows, by placing the command **MSAV** into the **AUTOEXEC.BAT** file.

VSAFE must be run separately, see earlier.

Summary

❑ Your **most important line of defence** is to use only software that has come from a reputable source.

❑ Always keep several **System floppies** so that you can boot the computer from a disk that is free of any virus infection. This is particularly useful also to combat a virus infection of COMMAND.COM, because this file can be copied from the floppy.

❑ **MWAV** is the anti-virus program that can be used from within Windows. The corresponding DOS version is MSAV. Both use a file in common as a source of information on viruses, and this list file needs to be updated regularly.

❑ There is also a memory-resident program **VSAFE** that will detect attempts to alter the layout of the hard drive.

❑ **MWAV** and **MSAVE** allow you run either a detection sweep by itself, or to detect and remove in one operation.

❑ The **Options** of MWAV and MSAV allow you to be more or less strict about detecting changes that might indicate a virus problem.

Take note

At the time of writing, virus utility programs would detect a virus on Windows 95 files but not remove it. This is why no virus correcting software has been included.

By the time that Windows 95 has been established as long as Windows 3.1, it is likely that some effective software will have been developed.

10 A new drive

Replacing a drive

Not many years ago, a hard drive of 40 Mbyte was considered luxurious. Along came Windows 3 and suddenly 80 Mbyte was desirable, and soon became a minimum specification. At the time of writing, 360 Mbyte is considered to be a reasonable drive size, but what will you need next year?

The simplest and cheapest option is to use DriveSpace if you have not already done so. If you have used DriveSpace and you are still running out of space, another option is to link up to another machine which has spare space — such a machine need use only MS-DOS and Interlink, with the rest of the drive used for data.

The last option is to replace the hard drive or to add another hard drive.

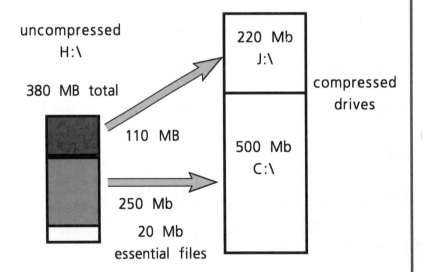

uncompressed
H:\

380 MB total

110 MB

250 Mb

20 Mb
essential files

220 Mb
J:\

compressed
drives

500 Mb
C:\

Possibilities

❑ If you are not using DriveSpace, think about it. You can use DriveSpace to get a compressed drive of up to 500 Mbyte, and if you use DriveSpace on drives of more than 250 Mbyte you can create one compressed drive of 500 Mbyte and another compressed drive which uses up the remainder. For example, from a 360 Mbyte drive you can use about 250 Mbyte for one compressed drive and about 110 Mbyte for another.

❑ Another option is to use an older machine with a hard drive, and connect it with a parallel cable, using Microsoft Interlink (supplied with MS-DOS).

Decisions

- You can get much more hard drive space for your money by adding another hard drive to your existing one.

- If your C:\ drive is more than two years old, it makes more sense to replace it with a larger capacity drive, or to make it the subsidiary drive.

- PC machines are the ultimate Meccano sets - a new hard drive can be plugged into place with very little effort and next to nothing in the way of technical knowledge. The main ability required is knowing that a square peg does not fit a round hole.

There are two hardware options as far as hard drive space is concerned. One is to replace the existing drive, the other is to add another drive.

Which way you proceed very much depends on how old your existing hard drive is, and its capacity. If, for example, you have a machine which is satisfactory, but which is cursed with only 40 Mbyte of elderly hard drive, then you should consider replacing this with a new drive of 180 Mbyte or more. You might also consider updating the whole machine, because if you need more drive space you probably need more memory and more speed.

If you are using a modern (486 or higher) machine with adequate memory (8 Mbyte or more) and a hard drive of 250 Mbyte or so, with DriveSpace, you should consider adding another drive. Hard drives are comparatively cheap now, so you can add another 250 Mbyte or more in this way.

Replacing a drive is the simplest option, because the new drive will almost certainly be of the same shape and size as the old one, and will fit into the same space. You hold it in place with four small bolts and connect with two plugs. Just remember to mark the top of each plug before you remove it from the old drive.

Take note

If you replace the C:\ drive, make sure that you have a floppy with the MS-DOS system tracks and the FORMAT command.

Adding a drive

Adding a drive is the more difficult of the options, because you need to find where to put the new drive.

Looking at how your existing hard drive is located will help you to decide where to put the new one. This is usually easier in a modern tower casing, and if you are using a portable machine you can forget about it unless your were apprenticed to a sardine-packer once.

Attaching a hard drive is not critical. The only vital point is that you must use the padded shock-proof mounting points that are provide. Never be tempted to use any other mounting points, and never drill the casing of a drive because you think it would make mounting easier.

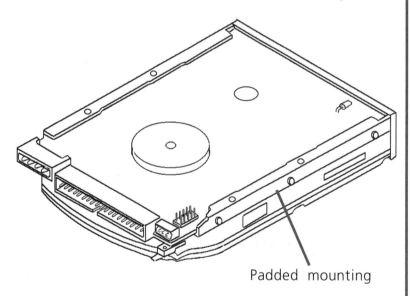

Padded mounting

1 Make certain that the cables which connect to your existing hard drive have an additional connector. The power cable (small plug) will almost certainly have several more connectors. The data cable might not, and you also need to make sure that it is installed the right way round.

2 Tower cases often have several brackets for adding more drives – some units will house up to eight drives. Desktop cases can often make use of a 5.25" wide bay, and you will need an adapter (a metal cage) to fit the hard drive, because most hard drives are of 3.5" width.

But first.....

1 Check that the hard drive you intend to add is of the same general type as the existing one. For modern machines, this will be one of two types called IDE or SCSI.

2 Check that you have a data cable that supports two drives (it should have a spare connector).

3 Check the drive package to make sure you have mounting screws, any adapter that is needed, cables (if not already on the computer) and instructions. Check that you have the necessary tools - a Philips screwdriver (possibly a plain-head type) and a pair of tweezers are usually needed.

Do it yourself

If you want to read up about hard drives and how to install them in detail, take a look at the book called Build Your Own PC (from Heinemann-Butterworth). This book deals also with other upgrades, like adding memory, adding CD-ROM and even upgrading the main board.

Old machines (such as anything that uses the 8088, 8086 or 80286 processor) can be a pain to work on, because you cannot be sure that the hard drive will be one of the modern types. You would normally want to make a complete upgrade of such a machine, and it's often cheaper to buy a modern replacement. Take a look at advertisements from Morgan Computer Co. to find just how cheap a modern machine can be.

Some modern machines can cope with adding a drive without making any changes to settings. Most machines will require some changes, and the most common requirements are jumpers or switches on the new and existing drives, and the CMOS memory settings of the computer.

If in doubt, enquire of the makers (and the best of luck) and also from the suppliers of the new hard drive.

What to look for

There's a lot to consider when you are looking for a additional or new hard drive. Your safest bet is always to use a drive from the same manufacturer and of the same type – SCSI or IDE – as your existing drive.

- **Size** is probably the first consideration. A drive of 512 Mbyte is not expensive now, and this is the largest size that Windows 3.1 can cope with. Windows 95 can cope with drives of 2 Gbyte or more. You might never need this sort of capacity, particularly if you use DriveSpace.

- **Speed** is important. The speed of a disk is quoted in terms of average access time in milliseconds (ms) (thousandths of a second). Do not consider any hard drive that requires more than 16 ms, and if speed is very important to you, look for faster access times than this.

- A **built-in cache** can increase the effective speed of a drive, and is worth paying extra for.

Modern drives need no jumpers or software setup (see later) – you simply plug them in and switch on. They may need to be formatted using the same method as you would use for a floppy disk.

Notes

- ❏ It's easy to buy a hard drive. Look through the pages of magazines like PC Plus or Computer Shopper and you will find dozens of suppliers.

- ❏ Prices are lower than they have ever been, almost half of what they were a few years ago.

- ❏ You cannot mix drive types easily. If your PC uses an IDE type of drive you must also add a SCSI driver card if you want to add a SCSI drive.

- ❏ If a drive is described as EIDE it is compatible with IDE - the E means Extended.

Basic steps

Fitting

1 Check that any jumpers or switches (see later) are correctly set. Once the drive is in place these will usually be impossible to reach. Use tweezers to manipulate these devices.

2 If possible, plug in the cables before you fasten the drive in place. It's usually easier to check that the plugs are correctly fitted if you can move the drive around. Look on the data cable for the marking that distinguishes the number one line. The power plug will fit only one way round.

3 Place the screws by hand and tighten evenly. Check as you tighten the screws that the drive is positioned correctly.

A drive should never be mounted with its connectors facing vertically up or down, or sloping at an angle of more than 5° up or down. It can be placed flat, either way up, or on either side.

Unpack the drive carefully and read any accompanying manual carefully. Check that any adapter plate fits into the mounting bay on the casing, and that all bolts and cable adapters (if needed) are provided.

If the drive is going into a 5.25" bay, fasten it to its adapter, using the small screws that are provided to bolt into the mounting pads. Tighten these up evenly and not excessively.

Data cable connector

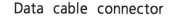
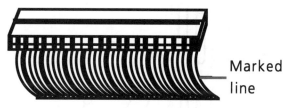

Marked line

rib

plug

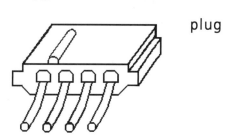

Jumpers

The jumpers of a hard drive are not of the woolly variety, but a way of switching connections so that the drive is correctly configured. A few modern drives are self-configuring, but the established system is that a drive can be configured as the only drive, as a master of two, or as a slave of two. If you don't get the settings correct you will be unable to use the drive.

The reason for needing this setting is that the data cable is common to both drives, so the differences between two hard drives have to be established at the drives themselves. If the cable connectors are labelled C: and D:, then no changes at the drives are needed.

1 If you have only one hard drive, set the jumpers at the position for One Drive. This is the setting that you need if you are replacing a hard drive by a larger one.

2 If you are adding a new drive to the existing one, you need to alter the jumpers on both.

3 The existing drive must be set as the Master of two.

4 The added drive must be set as the Slave of two.

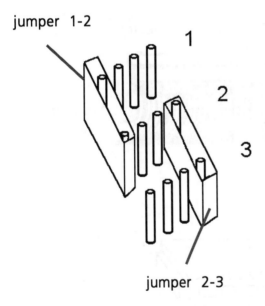

jumper 1-2

1

2

3

jumper 2-3

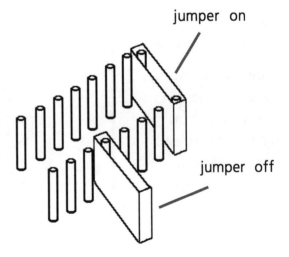

jumper on

jumper off

List

1 The jumpers are wrongly set

2 The data cable is incorrectly inserted into the socket.

3 You are using the wrong type of drive – IDE and SCSI are not interchangeable.

4 The software SETUP has not been altered (see later).

5 The power plug has not been inserted.

Tip

Use a spotlight and a magnifying glass to ensure that the data connector is correctly located.

What can go wrong?

One problem about adding a hard drive is that you will not know whether you have been successful or not until you come to use the drive.

The most common problem, which applies to adding a floppy drive as well, is that the data plug has not been inserted correctly. This plug uses two rows of miniature sockets which should line up with two rows of tiny pins on the drive. If the two are not perfectly lined up you can engage one set of pins but not the other, or you can have pins unconnected at either side. The drive can work only if all the pins are correctly connected.

It's not as easy as you might think, because you very often have to make the connections when you cannot see the plug or socket, hence the advice about trying to make connections before the drive is fixed in place.

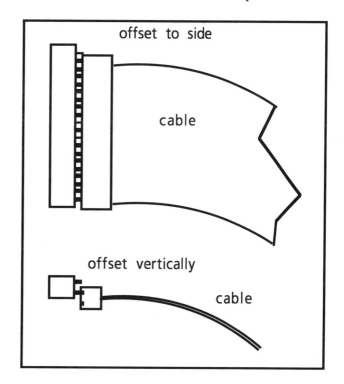

offset to side

cable

offset vertically

cable

The software setup

Some modern machines will accept a changed or added hard drive with almost nothing in the way of software changes, but it's much more likely that the CMOS setup will need to be changed.

Once again, some machines will sense the change and enter this SETUP screen automatically whenever you switch the machine on after making the change. The alternative is that you press some keys as you switch on — and only your manual for the computer will tell you which keys to press, because this varies from one machine to another. Typical methods are holding down Ctrl-Alt-Esc, or Ctrl-Alt-S while switching on.

```
          ***STANDARD SYSTEM PARAMETERS***

System Time:      hh:mm:ss      Numlock on at boot:   NO
System Date:      mmm dd, yyyy  Password:             N/A

Diskette A:       3.5", 1.44MB
Diskette B:       Not Installed   Cyl  Hd  Sec  Size
Hard Disk 1:      Installed       872  16   36   245
Hard Disk 2:      Not Installed
Base Memory:      640KB
Extended Memory:  7168KB
Video Card:       VGA/EGA
Keyboard:         Installed
CPU Speed:        Fast
```

Take note

Do not alter any other parts of the Setup unless you know what you are doing or are following instructions in a manual.

1 Enter the CMOS Setup screen, using whatever method is described in the manual for the computer.

2 You will see a list of system settings, which will include Hard Disk 1 and Hard Disk 2.

3 Enter the figures that are needed for the Hard drive you have just installed. If you have replaced an existing drive, alter the Hard Disk 1 settings. If you have added a drive, enter new figures for the Hard Disk 2 settings.

❏ These figures will be found on the documents that accompany your new hard drive.

4 Once you have altered the Setup, take the **Save and Exit** option.

Basic steps

1 Find what drive letter is being used. If you do not use DriveSpace you will almost certainly find that D:\ is used for a second hard drive. Since DriveSpace is not used when you add a drive, it will initially use the D:\ letter.

2 Format the new drive. The method of formatting a hard drive is exactly the same as it is for a floppy, but things are more complicated if you have replaced a drive rather than adding a drive.

3 If you have replaced your C:\ drive you must boot up from a floppy, and format the C:\ drive from this floppy.

Putting into service

When you replace a hard drive with a larger hard drive the new drive will use the same C: drive letter as the old one. When you add a hard drive, a new letter will be assigned. This is often D:\, but when you use DriveSpace on a second hard drive, you will find that the letter D:\ is used for the 'real' drive, and the compressed drive letter is G:\ or H:\ - you simply have to find what your computer allocates because it depends on what other equipment you have (a second floppy drive, a CD-ROM, a tape streamer etc.).

If you replace your C:\ drive, you will no longer have MS-DOS on the C:\ drive, so that you must boot the computer from a floppy disk. You should always keep several copies of floppies with the System tracks on them, and some essential command files such as FORMAT.COM. You can place this disk in the drive when you boot, make sure that you are logged and then use FORMAT C:\ to format your new hard drive.

If you have added a new drive, this will almost certainly be the D:\ drive, and it can be formatted using the FORMAT command in the older C:\ drive. Simply log on to the C: drive and use FORMAT D:\ to format the new drive.

Take note

Formatting a large hard drive can take some time.

Format and Unformat

The formatting of a hard drive (or of a floppy) can be reversed. If you want to ensure that all information on a drive is destroyed, you can use the /U addition to the FORMAT command. For example, FORMAT A: /U will format the floppy in the A: drive and ensure that no recovery of data is possible.

If the /U addition has not been used, it is often possible to restore a disk after formatting. This would be necessary if you found that the disk or drive you had just formatted had been filled with useful files. You might, for example, format your C: drive instead of the D: drive. It's unlikely, because you would be reminded of what you were doing, but no-one's perfect.

Take note

The safest way to use **UNFORMAT** initially is:

UNFORMAT D:\/TEST

which will check if the drive can be successfully unformatted, and will report what portion of the contents can be recovered.

❑ UNFORMAT cannot succeed if the **FORMAT /U** command has been used.

❑ UNFORMAT cannot restore files that were fragmented; saved to more than one set of locations on the hard drive.

❑ The sector size (the number of bytes for each storage unit) used on your hard disk must be 512, 1024, or 2048 bytes. This is something that should be stated in documents about your hard drive.

❑ You cannot use UNFORMAT on a drive that is remotely connected through a network.

❑ UNFORMAT must be used from MS-DOS, it cannot be used from Windows.

- A System floppy is one that has been formatted with the MS-DOS hidden files, so that it can be used to boot the computer.

- If, for example, the hard drive should fail to start some day, you can still boot from the System floppy and gain access to the computer, though not to the hard drive.

- If the system files on the hard drive become corrupted, you can gain access to the hard drive after booting from a floppy.

- If a virus infects your COMMAND.COM file, you can make a clean copy from the System floppy. This applies also to other important SYS files.

One of the most important safeguards against hard drive problems and virus infections is the possession of several System floppies. Once you have been using a hard drive for a time you tend to forget how important a System floppy is. Alternatively, if you have never used a floppy-only machine you may not know the importance of a System floppy.

You should make more than one System floppy. For peace of mind, I prefer to keep three, all in different places. Store the disks in cool dry places well away from magnets (and don't forget where you put them).

As well as making the disk a System one, you should save some other important files, such as the DRVSPACE files, and a few utilities.

autoexec.bat	drvspace.mr1	sys.com
command.com	emm386.exe	testdrv.com
config.sys	hhscand.sys	testdrv.doc
country.sys	io.sys	vmode.exe
diskmap.dat	keyb.com	
driver.sys	keyboard.sys	
drvspace.bin	keyclick.com	
drvspace.ini	msdos.sys	

Making the System disk

Always use floppies that you can rely on totally. For your Systems disks, use a surface scan of SCANDISK to check that the magnetic material is good enough for a disk which might save you from disaster.

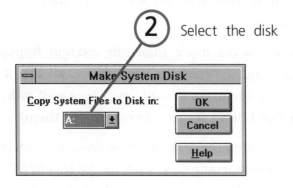

Select the disk

Take note

Do not use a DriveSpaced floppy as a System disk - it is not suitable because a system disk has to be used before the computer has loaded in the DriveSpace codes.

Label your System disks clearly and show the date of creating them.

If you change your DOS version, make new System floppies.

1 Insert the floppy into the drive.

2 **From DOS**, log to the C:\ drive or C:\DOS directory and type the command:

FORMAT A: /S

Or

From Windows, switch to **File Manager**. With the floppy in the A: drive, select **Disk – Make System Disk**, pick a disk and click on **OK**.

3 Wait until the formatting is complete and the system tracks have been added.

4 Copy over other important files, like the DRVSPACE files, and some utilities.

Basic Steps

Windows 95 System disk

1 Get a formatted 1.4 Mbyte floppy ready.

2 Click on the **Start** button and move the pointer to **Settings** and **Control Panel**. Click on this.

3 Double-click on **Add/ Remove Programs**.

4 Click on the **Startup Disk** tab.

5 Click **Create Disk**.

6 You will be asked to insert your Windows 95 No. 1 setup disk. If Windows 95 was installed from a CD-ROM, place it in its drive.

7 You will then be asked to insert a blank floppy which will become the Startup disk.

A System disk for Windows 95 is one that allows you to run MS-DOS if the computer for any reason cannot load Windows 95. This is a last line of defence that allows you to get to your files and, with luck, to run SCANDISK and remove any problem that has prevented Windows 95 from starting.

You normally create such a disk when Windows 95 is installed, but if you did not get one with your computer or you have lost it, here's how to make a new one.

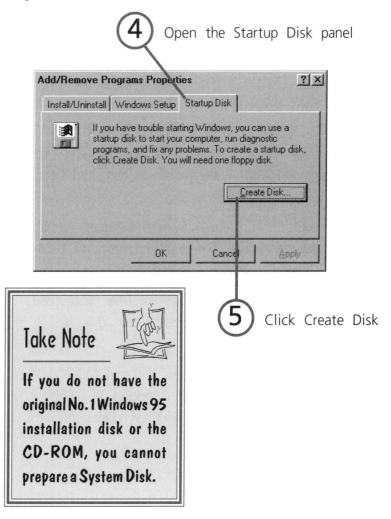

④ Open the Startup Disk panel

⑤ Click Create Disk

Take Note

If you do not have the original No. 1 Windows 95 installation disk or the CD-ROM, you cannot prepare a System Disk.

143

Summary

❑ The need for more hard drive space never ceases, and a hard drive of 350 Mbyte is now normal for a desktop computer.

❑ The easiest way of obtaining more space is to use **DriveSpace** on your present hard drive.

❑ The **other options** are to replace the whole computer, to replace the hard drive only, or to add another hard drive. The last is often best value for money if the rest of the computer is up to date.

❑ **Replacing a hard drive** is not a difficult action. Adding a new drive takes a little more planning.

❑ When any change is made to the hard drive system, the **CMOS setup** must be changed to correspond with the new disk size.

❑ A new hard drive may need to be formatted, using the normal **FORMAT** command. It can also be DriveSpaced after formatting.

❑ You should also prepare **System floppies**, which allow you to regain control in the event of hard-drive problems or virus infection.

❑ To create a **Windows 95 System Disk**, you need your original Windows 95 installation disk No. 1 (or the CD-ROM).

❑ The Windows 95 System Disk will run MS-DOS if your computer cannot start Windows 95. This allows you to access files and run diagnostic programs.

Glossary

Application A program for a particular purpose, such as word-processing or spreadsheet use.

Attribute A marker put into a filename so that the computer can act on it. e.g. the RO attribute makes a file read-only; it cannot be written to.

AUTOEXEC.BAT one of two important text files that is used to set up the computer for use each time it is switched on. The other file is **CONFIG.SYS**.

Boot To start or restart the computer either with the main switch or by using the key combination of [Ctrl]-[Alt]-[Del]. See also **reboot**.

Branch A disk directory which is connected to a main (root) directory or to another more important directory.

CONFIG.SYS A file of commands which install important programs that remain in the memory of the computer and control its actions.

Current In use. The current drive is the drive that you are using, and the current directory is the one that you are logged to and using.

[Ctrl]-[Alt]-[Del] The key combination that will reboot the computer. If you are running Windows you will need to use this key combination twice to reboot.

Default A choice that is made for you and which need only be acknowledged.

Defragment To reorganise the data on a disk so that each file is stored as a continuous whole, rather than being spread over several parts of the disk.

Enhanced mode The conventional method of running Windows on modern machines – older methods are now obsolete.

Extended memory The type used on a modern machine which contains more than 1 Mb of RAM memory. Any machine that runs Windows needs extended memory, usually at least a total of 4 Mbyte.

Macro A type of mini-program in the form of a text file that is used to automate the actions of a program.

MSD The Microsoft System Diagnostics program, used to deliver a report on your computer system.

Platter An aluminium disc coated with magnetic material. Several platters are used to make up a hard drive, with two heads used to read the two sides of each platter.

Reboot To restart a computer that has already been running, using the [Ctrl]-[Alt]-[Del] keys (soft reboot) or a separate Reset key (hard reboot). Many computers no longer use a Reset key.

Root The main directory of any disk or drive, accessed by using the drive letter alone.

Swap file A large file placed on the hard drive and used to contain programs and data that have been started but that Windows is not currently running.

Text file A file that can be edited by a word-processor, using only the codes for the letters, numbers and punctuation signs.

Index

Symbols

386SPART.PAR file, 79

A

Adding a drive, 132
Adding folder, Windows 95, 31
Advanced options, defragment, 71
Advanced options, Scandisk, 99
Advantages, hard drive, 2
Allocation units, 91
Anti-virus installation, 121
APPEND command, 22
Auto Arrange, 37
Automount, 82
Autoselection, backup, 46
Avoiding virus, 119

B

Backing up, 3
Backup on floppies, 40
Backup, Windows 95, 54
Bay, 132
Bomb, 119

C

Cache, Windows 95, 65
Cache, 61
Catalogue file, Windows 95, 56
CD command, 15
CD.. command, 10
Change directory, 16

Child, 10
CHKDSK utility, 91
Clean option, anti-virus, 122
Clearing scrap, 97
Clusters, loose, 68
CMOS setup, 138
Colorado Jumbo, 53
Compatibility test, 43
Compress new drive, 85
Compression ratio, 77
Compression, backup, 47
Configuring MWAV, 124
CVF, 78

D

Damaged files, 96
Data connector, 135
Default set, 48
Defragmenter, Windows 95, 70
Defragmenting, 66
Delete directory, Windows 3.1, 32
Delete folder, Windows 95, 33
Deleted files, 102
Deleting directory, 18
DELTREE command, 18
Detect option, anti-virus, 122
Diagram, tree, 8
Differential backup, 50
DIR command, 15
DIRCMD, 19
Directories, 6
Directory display, 19

147